25 ORIGINAL ORGANIZED CRIME CROSSWORD PUZZLES BY FORMER-MOBSTER-TURNED-AUTHOR SONNY GIRARD.

Sonny Girard

ISBN: 0-9821696-7-1
ISBN-13: 978-0982169674

TEST YOUR MOB KNOWLEDGE

Table of Contents

Sonny's Mob Crossword #1:

MOB 101 EDITION

Across
4. Bugsy's Vegas hotel
5. New Orleans mob boss
8. Killed outside Spark's
10. Joe Colombo's Italian organization (Abbr)
11. Helped WWII invasion of Sicily
12. This mob rat coined "Cosa Nostra" on TV
14. Second in command in mob hierarchy
17. Colombo predecessor
20. Turned on John Gotti
21. He hounded Capone
23. St. Valentine's Day Massacre city

Down
1. Lord High Executioner surname
2. 1900 New York Italian Detective
3. Genovese first name
6. 1957 mob convention site
7. Missing union boss
9. Reles fell from this hotel's window
12. Bugsy's moll
13. 1931 murderous Night of the...
15. Old time black gangster, Johnson
16. Site of Lepke execution
18. Chicago mob's name, the _____
19. Joe Gallo murder site
22. Mean Streets director

Sonny's Mob Crossword #2:

LAS VEGAS SPECIAL

Across:

4. Cash taken from casino profits for mobsters
8. Vegas killer, Frank, turned government witness
9. Put a million dollars in a glass case in his casino
12. Virginia Hill's nickname
15. Bugsy's partner Lansky
16. Next world class hotel built after the Flamingo
17. Sedway and Dalitz
18. Lefty Rosenthal's wife's first name
19. Caifano preceded Spilotro as Chicago mob's Vegas rep
20. Highway 91 known as
21. Las Vegas Mayor Goodman
22. List of Excluded People common name

Down:

1. Mobster Rick Rizzolo owned this famous strip club
2. Free trips to Vegas for gamblers
3. Bugsy director, Barry
5. Las Vegas airport
6. Legendary poker pro, Amarillo
7. Actor James Caan had one of these in Vegas
10. Casinos have none of these
11. Tony Spilotro's Vegas gang
13. Downtown Vegas' main casino street
14. Rat Pack member later had his own late night talk show

Sonny's Mob Crossword #3:

PROHIBITION EDITION

Across

2. New York Mayor, Jimmy
6. Fixed 1919 World Series
7. Prohibition Amendment number
9. Mob boss killed in Coney Island restaurant
12. Capone moniker
14. Alcohol-producing device
15. Presidential dad and Scotch bootlegger
16. Lucky mob leader
17. Bugsy Siegel's given name
20. This Act launched Prohibition
21. First FBI Chief
22. Homemade alcohol drink

Down

1. Female craze of the time
3. Capone headquarters
4. Brownsville gangster Amberg nickname
5. Killed in Palace Chophouse
6. 21st Amendment did this to Prohibition
8. Fitzgerald book about the era
10. Roaring Twenties film's star
11. Prohibition passed under this President
13. Last Prohibition President
14. Place to drink in the '20s
18. Name for those who sold unlawful alcohol
19. Capone nemesis

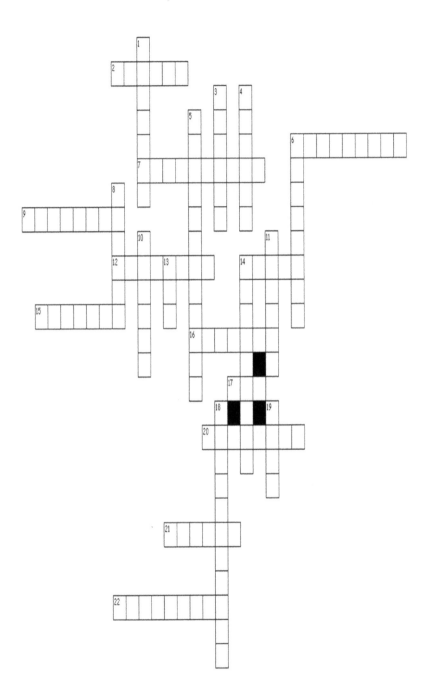

Sonny's Mob Crossword #4:

NEW YORK EDITION

Across

2. Shot at Manhattan rally of IACRL
7. Government tool to fight mob
8. Lepke's surname
11. Chicago mob boss born in Brooklyn
13. Crazy Joe Gallo killed here
15. Money lender's interest
17. "Three Finger Brown" Family name
18. Lord High Executioner
20. Lansky & Siegel original gang
22. Henry Hill's boss, Paulie
23. Boss abdicated to Arizona

Down

1. Known as the "Prime Minister"
3. Trial of mob bosses
4. Joe Pistone undercover name
5. Lanza ran Fulton Street Market
6. Bathrobe Boss
9. Little Flower Mayor smashed slots
10. Gotti's Manhattan social club
11. Gotti convicted of murdering boss Paul
12. Gallos rebelled against this boss
14. Stoolpigeon Abe Reles' moniker
16. NY Lt. Detective killed in Sicily
19. Brownsville Jewish gang of killers
21. Main Street of Little Italy

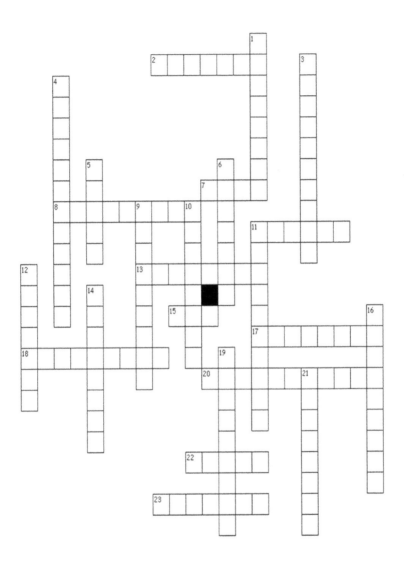

Sonny's Mob Crossword #5:

PUBLIC ENEMIES EDITION

Across

6. Lepke's partner
9. Known for his boyish looks
11. They made illegal alcohol
12. Walter Winchell arranged his surrender
13. Alvin robbed banks with the Barker Gang
14. Melvin led a squad that killed a Pretty Boy
16. FBI Director in '30s
20. Prison known as "The Rock"
21. Feds killed him when he left a movie theater
23. Drivers who waited in the car for robbers
24. Machine Gun Jack

Down

1. Scarface's brother Ralph's nickname
2. Gangster's machine gun
3. Studio famous for gangster films of the '30s
4. Lady in ___ set up a public enemy for Feds
5. Murderous pair of lovers
7. Movie about Feds who got Capone
8. This Bugs was missed on St. Valentine's Day
10. Joe Aiello warred with this famous mobster
15. Beatty who played Barrow on film
17. Prime targets for robbers in the 30s
18. Matriarch of a public enemy gang
19. Mr. Barrow's first name
22. Posters of criminals in post offices

Sonny's Mob Crossword #6:

BROOKLYN EDITION

Across

2. Lucchese turncoat Casso's nickname
7. Sammy the Bull's last name
9. Mustachio boss killed in Coney Island restaurant
11. Fat Roy DeMeo's lounge
12. Pretty left his dead victims on the street in laundry bags
13. This Murder Incorporated canary sang but couldn't fly
14. Larry Gallo strangled at this bar/nightclub
17. Funzi Tieri ran this Family
19. Joe Gallo's moniker
20. Mob hopefuls
21. Gotti "dry snitch" Willie Boy
22. Bonnano Family boss rolled over for Feds

Down

1. Colombo mob stoolpigeon helped FBI in Mississippi
3. Joe Doto's macho nickname
4. Known as the Lord High Executioner
5. This Brooklyn mob boss sent Al Capone to Chicago
6. Paul Sorvino played this real Paul in Goodfellas
7. Castellano's predecessor
8. Boss gunned down in front of a Manhattan steakhouse
10. Shylock's loan interest
15. Frank DeCicco blown up on 86th Street in this area
16. Murder Incorporated came from this Brooklyn area
17. South Brooklyn canal known for dumped bodies
18. Brooklyn's federal court's district

Sonny's Mob Crossword #7:

ITALY EDITION

Across

3. Sicilian mob's ruling commission
5. Author of "Gomorrah" in hiding
6. Tomasso testified against fellow Mafiosi
7. Vatican banker poisoned in his prison cell
9. Palermo's famous prison
10. Don Vito is Sicily's most venerated Mafia don
11. Mussolini's Iron Prefect, Cesare, persecuted Mafia
12. Organized crime of Naples
14. Group of former Mafiosi who testified at trial
16. Prime Minister, Giulio, accused of Mafia ties
17. Organized crime of Sicily
19. Michael's Sicilian wife in "The Godfather"
21. Salvatore Riina's nickname

Down

1. Murdered Mafia prosecutor, Giovanni
2. Italian banker hung under a London bridge
4. Lucky Luciano died in this Italian city
5. Organized crime of Puglia
8. 17 year old Sicilian girl who turned in Mafiosi
11. Trial of over 300 Mafiosi
13. Bandit, Salvatore, subject of Coppola film
14. American detective murdered in Sicily
15. Organized crime of Calabria
18. New York trial with a Sicilian connection
20. Calabrian mob bosses meet at the Sanctuary of Our Lady of

―――――

Sonny's Mob Crossword #8:

ATLANTIC CITY THEN & NOW EDITION

Across
3. To produce illegal alcohol
6. Mrs. Schroeder's first name in "Boardwalk Empire"
9. Nucky's real last name
11. "Boardwalk Empire" was filmed here
13. Nucky lived at this hotel
15. Racing Wire Erickson's first name
16. This mobster also had his honeymoon at the 1929 AC meeting
18. The Boardwalk was built to keep this out of hotel lobbies
20. Nucky "Thompson" actor
21. The first casino in the new AC, 1978
23. Alcohol smugglers' cars souped-up to outrun Feds led to these races
24. Directed first "Boardwalk Empire" episode

Down
1. Chicago rep at 1929 AC meeting
2. Nucky's political party
4. Joseph P. smuggled Scotch into the U.S.
5. The 1929 AC meeting formed a new mob organization called the
7. Nig represented Philadelphia in the 1929 AC meeting
8. Atlantic City inspired this board game
10. Nucky did time in this prison
12. These two Jewish "Gorilla Boys" attended the 1929 AC meeting
14. The real Nucky went to prison for this
17. The 20s are known as Atlantic City's _____ Age
19. Racing Wire Annenberg's first name
22. Philly mob's Nicky ran its business in the new AC

Sonny's Mob Crossword #9:

MOB BUSTERS EDITION

Across

3. Held mob hearings for FDR
5. Rudy's big trial was first to send many mob bosses to prison
8. Frank Costello appeared off camera before this Senate Committee
9. NY Police Commissioner became U.S. President
12. Al Capone nemesis
13. Recent large mob trial in Chicago
16. Racketeer Influenced and _____ Organizations
18. Il Duce's Mafia buster
19. Famous Palermo prison
20. First Director of the FBI
22. Manhattan's Federal Court District
23. Robert _____ wrote the RICO Act
24. Undercover agent Donnie Brasco's real name

Down

1. Mafia trial of hundreds in Sicily
2. U.S. detective murdered in Sicily, 1909
4. Newsman helped Lepke turn himself in to FBI
6. Brooklyn's Federal Court District
7. Excellent Cadavers filmed about this Italian prosecutor
10. Mobster first to name Cosa Nostra for Congressional Committee
11. Nemesis of murdered U.S. detective in Sicily, 1909
14. Melvin headed up squad that killed Dillinger
15. Al Capone's lawman brother
17. Prosecuted and convicted Lucky Luciano
21. Played Al Capone nemesis in Untouchables TV series

Sonny's Mob Crossword #10:

CHICAGO EDITION

Across

6. Handsome Johnny washed ashore in an oil drum
8. DeNiro played him in Casino
10. 2009 large Chicago mob trial
11. Capone accountant Guzik's nickname
13. Played Capone's nemesis in film The Untouchables
15. Capone foe George Moran's nickname
16. Mob boss Frank committed suicide
17. St. Valentine's Massacre took place here
19. Capone's lawman brother
21. Caifano's law enforcement first name

Down

1. This Nick was first made guy to testify against the Chicago mob
2. What killed Al Capone?
3. Chicago's Des Moine faction mob boss Louis Fratto's nickname
4. Tony's body found in Indiana cornfield
5. Chicago mob's name
7. Capone's movie moniker
9. Joey Lombardo's nickname
11. Chicago mob boss involved with CIA
12. Hitmen Anselmo and _____ killed by Capone
14. Last Chicago mob boss before Capone
15. Ralph Capone's nickname
18. Island prison where Big Al did time
20. Ran movie union in L.A. for Chicago mob
22. Big Tuna's real last name

Sonny's Mob Crossword #11:

BOSSES EDITION

Across

3. Joe Bonnano escaped with his life to this state
4. A scalp wound forced this mob prime minister to retire
6. Chicago boss committed suicide
10. Eboli's Irish handle
12. Boston's legendary boss, Raymond
15. Bonnano boss became rat
16. Carlo succeeded Albert
18. Bonnano boss Rusty's surname
19. Carlos ran New Orleans with an iron fist
21. Des Moines mob boss Lou Fratto's nickname
22. The Gentle Don killed in Philadelphia
23. Nicky ran bloody Philadelphia crew

Down

1. Gotti's sartorial nickname
2. Brothers preceded Anastasia as family rulers
4. Missed his last meal at Spark's Steakhouse in 1985
5. Joey the Clown's real name
7. Fought war with rebellious Gallo Brothers
8. Lucky's family now carries this former boss's name
9. Tommy Lucchese known as
11. Brooklyn exile ran the Chicago mob
13. Chicago's Big Tuna
14. Jersey boss DeCavalcante was known as
17. Gotti underboss skated on murders to testify
20. Momo killed while cooking in his kitchen

Sonny's Mob Crossword #12:

TOUGH JEWS EDITION

Across

3. Detroit's Jewish-led mob
5. Masseria killer known for his hair color
6. Cleveland mob's Milton was liaison to Teamsters
7. Dutch Schultz's right hand man, Bo
9. Phil Strauss of Brooklyn nicknamed for this city
12. Brooklyn area known for old time Jewish killers
13. Jewish Moe known as Mr. Las Vegas
14. Arnold thought to have fixed 1919 World Series
16. DeNiro played him in Scorsese's Casino
19. Lepke and Gurrah were known as
20. Gypsy Rose Lee's gangster beau, _____ Gordon
21. Gurrah's son ran junkets to Vegas
22. Nickname of stoolpigeon Abe Reles

Down

1. Jewish killers under Anastasia's command
2. Lepke and Gurrah killed this Little Augie to take over
3. City repped by Nig Rosen at 1929 Atlantic City mob convention
4. This Louis was so ugly, he was called Pretty
8. Anastasia's Jewish killers hung out in this candy store
10. Ben Siegel's partner
11. L.A. mobster escaped numerous murder attempts
15. Abe Reles couldn't fly from this hotel's window
17. Hotel owner Ian Shrager's dad's nickname
18. Character shot through eyeglasses in Godfather
20. Mendy from Brooklyn and Hymie from Chicago

Sonny's Mob Crossword #14:

FILM & TV EDITION

Across

5. Paulie Walnuts' only food when stuck in the snow
8. Mobster Christopher Walken gets his finger chopped off in this movie
10. Steve Martin gets this built in "My Blue Heaven"
11. The brothers were buried here in "Casino"
15. Real ex-cop Dennis Farina played a police lieutenant in this TV series
16. In "Mean Streets," Meatloaf calls DeNiro & pals "mooks" here
18. Eric Roberts gets this cut off in "The Pope of Greenwich Village"
19. Alec Baldwin's nickname in "Married to the Mob"
21. Danny DeVito tells the story of his pal, Jack Nicholson, in this film
22. Armand Assante portrayed this famous mobster for HBO
23. What Roberto Benigni steals in "Johnny Stecchino"

Down

1. Eliot Ness in the TV series "Untouchables"
2. Comedian played mobster Loggia's sidekick in "Innocent Blood"
3. DeNiro's nickname in "Once Upon a Time in America"
4. Harvey Keitel's character in "Mean Streets"
6. The vegetable Dennis Hopper calls Chris Walken in "True Romance"
7. Directed "Once Upon a Time in America"
9. Neville Brand, Jason Robards, and Ben Gazzara all played him
12. Sleeps with the fishes
13. Ken Wahl was an undercover cop in this TV series
14. Young Vito Corleone kills him in the hallway outside his apartment
17. Keitel played _____ to Beatty's Bugsy Siegel
19. Rocky Sullivan in the original "Angels with Dirty Faces"
20. Richard Grieco plays Bugsy Siegel in this film

Sonny's Mob Crossword #15:

MOB CITIES EDITION

Across

1. Whitey went on the lam from Boston for years
5. NY borough was site of a mob meeting called "Little Apalachin"
6. Angelo Bruno and Nicky Scarfo were bosses here
9. Mafia suspects were hung by citizens in this Southern city in 1890
12. Home city of the Krays
15. Mafiosi Bernardo Provenzano & Toto Riina from this Sicilian city
18. Lucky Luciano snuck out of Italy for meeting here
19. Borough where Paul Castellano was murdered
21. Machine gun attack on Capone in this Chicago suburb
22. Family Secrets trial held here

Down

1. Area home of Brooklyn's Russian mob
2. Bonnano southwest retreat
3. This Joseph hosted an Apalachin, NY mob meeting in 1957
4. Russell was the boss of Scranton, PA
7. Rizzuto Family mobsters were recently killed in this Canadian city
8. City featured in the book and film "Gomorrah"
10. Home of the so called Mickey Mouse Mafia
11. 'Ndrangheta-honored Sanctuary of Our Lady of Polsi location
13. Canadian city controlled by Calabrian-run mob
14. City famous for the old Purple Gang
16. Chicago mobster "Cockeyed Lou" ran Des Moines mob
17. Ucciardone prison is in this city
20. First Family of the Tampa mob
21. Father of Kansas City mob family, Nick

Sonny's Mob Crossword #16:

STOOLPIGEONS EDITION

Across

2. Bonanno informer Richard Cantarella's nickname
4. His name became synonymous with mob rat after McClellan Hearings
6. Dominick Montiglio ratted out this Gambino Captain uncle of his
8. DiLeonardo was godfather to Junior Gotti's second son before ratting
11. "Junior" Pagan ratted out his father-in-law discussed on this TV show
14. Sopranos stoolie character killed on a boat
17. Frank Calabrese Jr. testified in the Family Secrets trial in this city
18. "Fish" Cafaro testified against this mob family in the late 1980s
20. Newark mob boss and rat Anthony Accetturo's nickname
21. Chris was Miami celebutante before ratting out his old pals
22. Colombo mobster Maragni was upped to captain before rolling over

Down

1. DeCavalcante mob rat "Vinny Ocean" busted in strip club in this city
2. Vatican banker Michele was poisoned in his prison cell after threatening to rat
3. Murder Inc stoolie Reles flew out the window of this hotel
5. Fat Pete testified against Lucchese mobsters after a failed attempt on his life
7. Lucchese boss and rat Anthony Casso's nickname
9. Mob Wives' Karen Gravano's turncoat father
10. Known as The Grim Reaper, this Colombo gunman died of AIDS
12. Stoolpigeon boss Joe Massino ran this mob family
13. Julius Bernstein who rolled on Genovese union deals was known as
15. Philly acting boss Ralph joined Team America
16. Michael Franzese testified against this entertainment businessman
19. Whitey Bulger's informant partner Steve Flemmi known as The
21. Fat Vinnie Teresa turned on his Boston mob boss Raymond

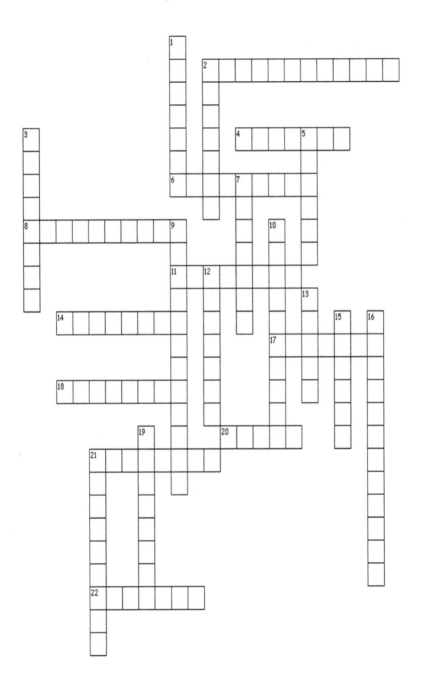

Sonny's Mob Crossword #17:

BOOKS EDITION

Across

5. "The Valachi Papers" was penned by
6. "Mob Over Miami" covers nightclub celeb turned mob rat Chris
7. Title of Robert Lacey's biography of Meyer Lansky
9. Leonard Katz's "Uncle Frank" is about
11. Harvey Aronson's story of a rogue N.J. mob crew
15. "Making the Wiseguys Weep" is the biography of singer Jimmy
16. "Unless They Kill Me First" tells of attempts on life of Vinnie The Cat
17. "Mob Princess" is the story of Antoinette
18. "A Man of Honor" tells the story of NY mob boss Joe
20. "Cigar City Mafia" is about the mob in this city
21. This Michael dictated "Quitting the Mob"
22. Turkus & Feder's book about Brownsville killers Reles, Strauss, etc.
23. T.J. English tome covering a mid-Manhattan crew of Irish mobsters

Down

1. "Mafia Kingfish" is the life story of New Orleans mob boss
2. Lynda Milito's book about her life married to a Gambino mobster
3. Dean Jennings' book "We Only Kill Each Other" is about
4. "Excellent Cadavers" is about murdered Sicilian magistrate Giovanni
5. "Revolt in the Mafia" is about the Gallo Brothers' war against Joe
8. Arrigo Petacci's book about Italian-American detective killed in Sicily
10. Roberto Saviano's book about the Neapolitan Camorra
12. Nick Pileggi's book was the basis for the film "Goodfellas"
13. He wrote "The First Family" about the early Sicilian Mafia in the U.S.
14. "This Family of Mine" was written by John Gotti's daughter
19. Jerry Capeci's "Murder Machine" is about

Sonny's Mob Crossword #18:

ACTORS EDITION

Across

2. Harvey Keitel played Mickey Cohen in this film
3. She played Peter Greene's moll girlfriend in The Mask
4. A wounded Edward G. Robinson hides here in Brother Orchid
5. Roberto starred in Italian mob comedy Johnny Stecchino
6. Andy Garcia played Lucky Luciano in this film
7. James Woods' character in Once Upon a Time in America
8. He played Lefty Ruggiero in Donnie Brasco
12. This Yankee Doodle Dandy star was known for gangster roles
14. Talia Shire's first name in The Godfather
15. Brando parodied his Godfather role in The _____
16. Chris Walken gives Dennis a cigarette before shooting him in True Romance
17. Danny and Joe Piscopo play small time hoods in the comedy Wise Guys
18. Steven Seagal was out for this in his Brooklyn mob-set film
21. Played the mob father in Mickey Blue Eyes

Down

1. Lenny Montana's character has a last drink at the bar in Godfather
5. Chazz Palminteri played local mob boss Sonny in this film
8. Michelle was Married to the Mob
9. Chazz Palminteri played magistrate Giovanni in Excellent Cadavers
10. DeNiro played Johnny Boy in Scorsese's 1973 film
11. Rod Steiger, Neville Brand, and Ben Gazzara all played him
13. Anthony Quinn played a Gambino underboss in this HBO film
19. Played Vinnie Terranova in the TV series Wiseguy
20. Actor Tony Sirico's nickname on Sopranos
22. She got a grapefruit facial in The Public Enemy

Sonny's Mob Crossword #19:

MURDERS EDITION

Across

1. Fat Roy DeMeo murdered victims at this Flatlands lounge
3. Gotti underboss Frankie DeCicco's car was blown up in this borough
5. Murdered Genovese acting boss Tommy Ryan's real last name
10. Only American detective ever killed overseas in the line of duty
11. Vatican banker Michele was poisoned in Italian prison cell
12. Dutch Schultz murdered in this NJ chop house
14. This Brooklyn stoolpigeon died from fall out of a hotel window
15. Chicago's St. Valentine's Day Massacre took place in this location
18. Chicago-L.A. mobster Johnny washed up to the beach in an oil drum
19. Arnold Schuster, killed on Anastasia's order, worked as a
21. Joe the Boss's rival was murdered in his office

Down

1. Carmine was murdered in restaurant garden chomping on a cigar
2. The Clutch Hand was known to murder victims in a Harlem stable
4. Chicago mob boss Momo killed in his basement
6. Vanished Genovese bigwig Anthony Strollo's moniker
7. "Godfather's" Sonny Corleone was killed here
8. "God's Banker" found hanging from a London bridge
9. Paul Castellano was murdered in front of this steak house
10. Angelo Bruno was murdered mob boss of what city?
11. Benjamin shot through a window while reading a newspaper
13. Famously killed in barber's chair
16. Second Sicilian prosecutor, Paolo, blown up within two months of Falcone
17. Went to electric chair for ordering trucker Joe Rosen's murder
20. Clam house where Joey Gallo was killed

Sonny's Mob Crossword #20:

ALPHABET EDITION

(1 answer for each letter; no Q or X)

Across

2. Mob's rule of silence
5. Tommy Ryan's real last name
7. Gypsy Rose Lee's gangster beau Mr. Gordon
8. Brownsville, Brooklyn gangsters incorporated this crime
12. Tony the Ant buried in a cornfield in "Casino"
14. Federal law aimed at the mob
16. Paolo Vaccarelli was this formerly Irish gang's first Italian leader
18. This Vincent was known as Mad Dog
19. Palermo's famous prison
20. Luciano snuck off to a 1946 meeting in this city
21. Tommy was killed with Paul Castellano
22. Nick Civella was this city's mob boss

Down

1. His name was synonymous with stoolpigeon after his 1962 testimony
3. Capone predecessor Johnny
4. Black Harlem gangster Bumpy
6. Jersey mobster Longy
9. Joe Zerilli was this city's mob boss
10. New York detective murdered in Sicily in 1909
11. Capone underling Jake Guzik was known as
13. Meyer got the boot from this country
15. Site of mass "Mafia" lynching in 1891
17. Mobster Socks and singer Mario
23. Luciano pal Joe Doto's taken name
24. Japan's organized crime group

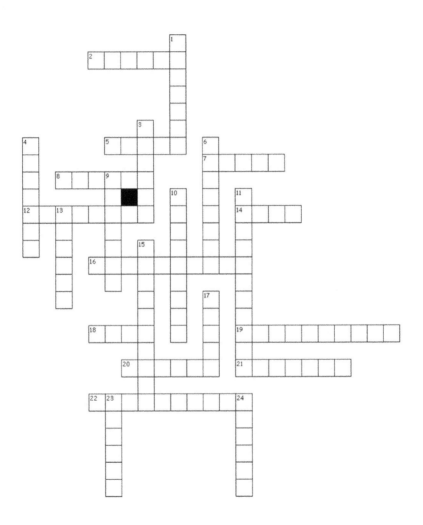

Sonny's Mob Crossword #21:

APHABET EDITION 2

(1 answer for each letter; no Q or X)

Across:

3. Gaspipe's surname
6. The real Nuckie's last name portrayed in HBO's Boardwalk Empire
9. Chicago's Momo
12. Joey the Clown's last name
13. Calabrian Mafia-type organization
14. Maxi-Processo Mafia trial was in this city
16. Known as the Mad Hatter or Lord High Executioner
17. Free trips to Vegas for high rollers
18. Dutch Schultz's death saved this lawman's life
22. Popular card game among Little Italy mobsters
23. Bugsy's hotel

Down:

1. Irish gang from New York's Hell's Kitchen
2. This Carlos ran the New Orleans mob with an iron fist
4. Whitey Bulger's home town
5. Robert Stack played Elliot Ness in this TV show
7. This Dion was shot to death in his Chicago flower shop
8. Gotti's home area
10. Frank Costello appeared off camera before this Senate Committee
11. Bonnano boss Rusty's last name
15. Brooklyn mob boss Frankie sent Capone to Chicago
19. This Monk led a gang of killers that opposed the Five Pointers
20. Loan shark interest
21. Lepke met his fate at this prison
24. Acronym for the ethnic organization Joe Colombo founded

NOTE: There are two acceptable spellings for **#24 Across**; only one fits in this puzzle

Sonny's Mob Crossword #22:

ALPHABET EDITION 3

(1 answer for each letter; no Q or X)

Across

5. Blue Jaw member of Murder Incorporated
9. Abe Reles' nickname
10. Claire Sterling's classic book on the international reach of the Mafia
12. Prosecutor Giovanni blown up in his car in Sicily
13. Tough Tony Anastasia ran this union for pier workers
15. Crazy Joe Gallo met his end at this Little Italy clam house
16. This Walter turned Lepke over to J. Edgar Hoover
17. Jewish Arnold mentored Lucky and Meyer
21. Cockeyed Lou Fratto ran this city for the Chicago Outfit
22. Captured Sicilian Mafia boss Provenzano
24. Three Finger Brown's mob family

Down

1. Site of 1957 mobster raid in Upstate New York
2. This Roselli made the wiseguys cry
3. Chin's first name
4. This boss was called The Beast by fellow Sicilian Mafiosi
6. Murder Inc's Phil Strauss associated with this city
7. Mario Puzo's "The Sicilian" was about bandit Salvatore
8. Actor Burt played mob guys from Pope of Greenwich Village to Sopranos
11. Lepke's partner Gurrah's last name
14. Neapolitan Mafia
18. Al Capone's lawman brother Two Gun's new last name
19. Judith dated JFK and Chicago mob boss Momo Giancana
20. This burning ship forced the Navy to ask Luciano for help in WWII
23. Big Jack took over for Monk Eastman and got killed on trolley

© 2012 R.I.C.O. Entertainment, Inc./All Rights Reserved.

Sonny's Mob Crossword #23:

COLOMBO FAMILY EDITION

Across

4. He did a benefit concert at MSG for Colombo's organization
5. This Rabbi Meir rallied with Joe Colombo
8. "Godfather II" strangling happened to Larry Gallo in this Brooklyn bar
9. Joe Colombo spent his days at this Bensonhurst real estate office
11. Colombo forced this film to drop Mafia references
12. Joe Gallo's pal Pete shot in the ass at Umberto's
13. Profaci stalwart Salvatore Mussachia's Arabian nickname
15. Profaci had a thief killed for robbing this place
16. Puzo made Luca Brasi sleep with the fishes after this real guy's death
18. The Gallo-Profaci War started after his murder
19. Joe Colombo informed him of Bonanno plot to murder him
20. Big Dino and Frankie Blue Eyes are both Colombo
21. Little Italy restaurant where Crazy Joe Gallo was murdered
22. This Police Inspector wrote "Revolt in the Mafia"
23. Profaci operated in this city before moving to NY

Down

1. Colombo held rallies at this Manhattan location
2. First family boss Joe Profaci was called the King of this product
3. Joe Gallo went to jail for threat made in this Little Italy restaurant
6. Colombo had this spicy TV ad removed as offensive to Italians
7. Hugh Macintosh's nickname
10. Profaci Consigliere Charles LoCicero's nickname
14. Colombo captain Greg played double role as killer and FBI informant
16. This Jerome shot Joe Colombo at the second Unity Day Rally
17. This Colombo turncoat testified about the Joey Gallo murder

Sonny's Mob Crossword #24:

LUCCHESE FAMILY EDITION

Across

2. "Mr. Gribbs" led the family after Lucchese passed away
5. Anthony Casso's street name
9. Lucchese backed the Gallos in their war with this boss
12. Lucchese boss during 1970s to '80s _____ Corallo
14. Johnny Dio died in this prison
15. Lucchese acting boss _____ D'Arco testified for the Feds
16. Lucchese sat on this executive board
18. Tommy Lucchese nickname
19. "Gribbs" went to prison for his connection this famous drug case
22. Nick wrote the script for "Goodfellas" and the book it's based on
23. Ernest Volkman's book on the Lucchese Family destruction
25. Corallo went to prison for bribing this NY Water Commissioner

Down

1. Lucchese infiltrated NY airport that later changed name to Kennedy
3. This Vic made Anthony Casso his underboss
4. The film "Goodfellas" is based on this book
6. Informant Fat Pete's girth kept bullets from killing him
7. Sorvino's Paul Cicero in "Goodfellas" was modeled after this Paul
8. Boss Corallo's famously bugged automobile
10. Johnny Dio's thought to have ordered acid thrown newsman Victor's face
11. Corallo's chauffeur Sal was also recorded on the car tapes
13. Union Lucchese was best known for his association with
17. He played real life Lucchese killer Tommy DeSimone in "Goodfellas"
20. Tommy Lucchese died of this
21. This NY Mayor Vincent was a good friend of Lucchese's
24. Jimmy the Gent's last name

Sonny's Mob Crossword #25:

GENOVESE FAMILY EDITION

Across

2. This Willie got Sinatra's contract from Tommy Dorsey at gunpoint
3. Acting boss Thomas Eboli's nickname
5. Trigger Mike's last name
7. Vincent Alo's nickname
8. The Family began with Giuseppe Morello in this part of NY
10. Lucky Luciano was deported to this Italian city
12. The government asked Luciano for help when this ship burned
14. Genovese threw a man off a roof so he could marry his wife ____
16. Luciano saved this prosecutor's life by ordering Dutch Schultz killed
18. Prostitute who testified against Luciano
20. Became a rat when he thought Genovese wanted him killed
22. The name of Gigante's social club
24. Chin Gigante's first name

Down

1. Chin was accused of wounding this acting family boss
4. Tony Bender disappeared from this New Jersey city
6. Luciano's man who controlled the piers for him
9. Lansky's brother who brought Waxey Gordon's records to the Feds
11. Chin's sartorial de rigueur
13. Lucky Luciano was in the bathroom when his boss got killed
15. Genovese fled to Italy to avoid being charged with his murder
17. Vito said to have ordered newsman's murder as a favor to Mussolini
19. He went to prison on the Commission Case as Genovese boss
21. Lucky got a heart attack and died at this location
23. Luciano's co-defendant Little Davey

Sonny's Mob Crossword #26:

ROARING TWENTIES EDITION

Across:

4. Capone killer partners Anselmi and
6. The Volstead Act ushered in this period
9. This duo murdered Little Augie Orgen to take over his gang
10. Socks Lanza organized this NY fish market
14. They manufactured illegal booze
15. 1939 film "The Roaring Twenties" starred Cagney and this male star
17. He had Vito Cascio Ferro arrested in a Sicilian Mafia purge
20. Vito Cascio Ferro sent this Salvatore to unify NY Italian gangsters
22. Moses Annenberg takes over this thoroughbred information service
23. Bootlegger Joe's son would someday be President
24. Illegal drinking establishment of the day

Down:

1. Joe Batters' real last name
2. This ex-cop and author Rick's family ran the Cleveland mob
3. Stephanie St. Clair was the numbers queen in this NY area
5. Paul Muni starred in this 1932 film named for Al Capone
7. Mob financier Arnold killed in 1928
8. His men were killed in the St. Valentine's Day Massacre
11. The name of Chicago's organized crime mob
12. Diamond got his nickname for outrunning a murder attempt in 1927
13. Modern Syndicate formed at a meeting in this beachfront location
16. John Perona's speakeasy would later become an elite NY nightclub
18. This Brooklyn mob leader sent Capone to Chicago after a killing
19. North Side Gang shot up this Cicero hotel trying to kill Capone
21. This Englishman known as The Killer ran Harlem's Cotton Club

MOB CROSSWORD ANSWERS

ANSWERS

MOB CROSSWORD #1

Mob 101 Edition

ACROSS:

4. FLAMINGO – Bugsy named his Las Vegas hotel after his girlfriend, Virginia Hill, who was nicknamed "Flamingo" for her long legs.

5. MARCELLO – Carlos Marcello ran New Orleans organized crime for more than thirty years, and is believed by many to have been part of a conspiracy in the murder President Kennedy.

8. CASTELLANO – Paul Castellano was the boss of the Gambino Family when he was gunned down by John Gotti's shooters as he left his car for a dinner meeting at Spark's Steak House.

10. IACRL – Mob boss Joe Colombo formed the Italian American Civil Rights League after his son was arrested for melting down U.S. coins for the silver.

11. LUCIANO – Lucky Luciano helped the U.S. Army invade Sicily by sending word to the island to welcome them. He was released from prison early and deported as a result of his aid.

12. VALACHI – Joe Valachi was the first member to testify to the existence of organized crime families. He coined the name "Cosa Nostra" in televised McClellan Committee hearings in 1963.

14. UNDERBOSS – Mob families were formed on the style of the Roman Legions. The boss is followed by an underboss then other positions down to made men and associates at the bottom.

17. PROFACI – Joseph Profaci was the first boss of what later became known as the Colombo Crime Family. He died of cancer in 1962.

20. SAMMYTHEBULL – Salvatore "Sammy the Bull" Gravano was John Gotti's underboss. He became a witness for the government after he and Gotti were arrested on murder charges.

21. NESS – Eliot Ness was a Prohibition agent, famous as the leader of a legendary team of law enforcement agents nicknamed the Untouchables that focused on Al Capone in Chicago.

23. CHICAGO – On Valentine's Day, 1929, Capone gunmen murdered seven of Bugs Moran's men in a garage. The main target, Moran, missed the event.

DOWN:

1. ANASTASIA – Albert Anastasia was known as both the Mad Hatter and the Lord High Executioner of organized crime.

2. PETROSINO – Joseph Petrosino was a famous crime fighter in New York at the turn of the Twentieth Century.

3. VITO – Vito Genovese took over the family previously run by Lucky Luciano and Frank Costello. That family bears his name till today.

6. APALACHIN – On November 14, 1957, police conducted a raid on the Upstate New York home of Joseph Barbara, during which they discovered and arrested major mob figures.

7. HOFFA – Jimmy Hoffa tried to regain his position as head of the Teamsters after leaving prison. He went to a meeting on July 30, 1975 and was never seen again.

9. HALFMOON – Murder Incorporated turncoat Abe "Kid Twist" Reles fell or was thrown from a sixth floor window of Coney Island's Half Moon Hotel while under police protection.

12. VIRGINIAHILL – Virginia was the love of Bugsy Siegel's life. He was shot to death in her Beverly Hills home.

13. VESPERS – On September 10-11, 1931 a number of "Moustache Petes" were murdered across the country to make way for the new organized crime structure. It is known as the "Night of the Vespers."

15. BUMPY - Ellsworth Raymond "Bumpy" Johnson was an African-American mob boss and bookmaker in New York City's Harlem. He was the main Harlem associate of the Genovese crime family.

16. SINGSING – Louis "Lepke" Buchalter was electrocuted at Sing Sing prison for the murder of union gadfly Joe Rosen on March 4, 1944.

18. OUTFIT – Unlike New York, Chicago has only one mob family, known as "The Outfit."

19. UMBERTOS – Joey Gallo and his group went to Little Italy's Umberto's Clam House after a night of partying to celebrate his 43rd birthday, where he was shot to death by Colombo loyalists.

22. SCORSESE – Martin Scorsese directed the 1973 film "Mean Streets," about Little Italy wannabe mobsters, starring Robert DeNiro and Harvey Keitel.

ANSWERS

MOB CROSSWORD #2:

Las Vegas Special

ACROSS:

4. SKIM – From the first time profits were made in Las Vegas casinos, money was taken off the record, or "skimmed," and sent back east to organized crime leaders.

8. CULLOTTA – Crew member Frank Cullotta became a government witness against his boss, Tony "The Ant" Spilotro.

9. BINION – Though fellow gambler Joe W. Brown was the front man because of Benny Binion's federal conviction, Benny engineered the late 1950s world famous display of one million dollars cash in his downtown Vegas "Binion's Horseshoe" casino.

12. FLAMINGO – Bugsy Siegel's mistress, Virginia Hill, was known as "The Flamingo" for her long legs.

15. MEYER – Known for his financial skills, Meyer Lansky was partners with Bugsy Siegel from their early days as namesakes of the Bug & Meyer gang.

16. DESERTINN – Originally known as Wilbur Clark's Desert Inn, it was taken over by Moe Dalitz and the Cleveland mob when Clark ran out of money before its completion.

17. MOES – Moe Dalitz ran the Desert Inn for the Cleveland mob, while Moe Sedway, along with Gus Greenbaum, took over the Flamingo Hotel for the New Yorkers only minutes after Bugsy Siegel was murdered in Los Angeles.

18. GINGER – Lefty Rosental's wife Geri was known as "Ginger," and was portrayed by Sharon Stone in Martin Scorsese's film, "Casino."

19. MARSHALL – Chicago mobster Marshall Caifano was tabbed as the boss of the Outfit's Las Vegas operations in 1951, and held that position until succeeded by Tony "The Ant" Spilotro twenty years later.

20. THESTRIP - The Las Vegas Strip is an approximately 4.2-mile stretch of Las Vegas Boulevard South, or Highway 91, where most of the best known casino hotels are located.

21. OSCAR – Former mob lawyer Oscar Goodman became the Mayor of Las Vegas in 1999 and kept the position for twelve years.

22. BLACKBOOK – Known as the Black Book, it is actually the "List of Excluded Persons" and has a silver binder. It lists organized crime figures who are not allowed in Vegas casinos.

DOWN:

1. CRAZYHORSETOO – Modeled after Las Vegas' original "Crazy Horse Saloon," the strip club was taken over by U.S. Marshalls after owner Rick Rizzolo was convicted of racketeering.

2. JUNKETS – Chartered planes were used for free trips for gamblers that included room, food, drink, shows, and more in Vegas hotels, depending on how high a roller a guest was.

3. LEVINSON – Barry Levinson directed the 1991 film of Bugsy Siegel's time in Las Vegas, "Bugsy," starring Warren Beatty, Annette Bening, and Harvey Keitel.

5. MCCARRAN – Named for Nevada Senator Pat McCarran, the airport's name was changed from McCarran Field to McCarran International Airport in 1968.

6. SLIM – Amarillo Slim was a professional poker player who won the World Series of Poker main event in 1972 and was inducted into the Poker Hall of Fame in 1992.

7. HONEYMOON – James Caan starred as gambler Tommy Korman in Andrew Bergman's 1992 film, "Honeymoon in Vegas."

10. CLOCKS – Like windows, there are no clocks in Vegas casinos to encourage the uninterrupted action of gamblers.

11. HOLEINTHEWALL – Tony Spilotro's crew of burglars was known as the "Hole in the Wall Gang."

13. FREMONT – Downtown Las Vegas' main street, Fremont Street, houses legendary casinos like Binion's Horseshoe, the Golden Nugget, and Four Queens.

14. BISHOP – Comedian and Rat Pack member Joey Bishop launched a late night show on ABC, "The Joey Bishop Show," which competed with Johnny Carson's "Tonight Show" for two years. His sidekick was Regis Philbin.

ANSWERS

MOB CROSSWORD #3:
Prohibition Edition

ACROSS:

2. WALKER – James "Jimmy" Walker was Mayor of New York City during the last half of Prohibition. He was forced to resign over a corruption scandal during his term.

6. ROTHSTEIN – Though Rothstein is widely believed to have had his agents fix the 1919 World Series between the Chicago White Sox and Cincinnati Reds, a grand jury could find no link between him and the scandal.

7. EIGHTEENTH – The Constitutional Amendment prohibiting the "...manufacture, sale, or transportation of intoxicating liquors within, the importation thereof into, or the exportation thereof from the United States," was ratified in January, 1919.

9. MASSERIA – On April 15, 1931, Joe "The Boss" Masseria was gunned down while eating and playing cards in the Nuova Villa Tammaro restaurant in Coney Island to end the Castellammarese War between him and Salvatore Maranzano.

12. SCARFACE – Al Capone got the nickname from a facial scar resulting from having been cut during a brawl in a Brooklyn bar where he worked as a bouncer in his early years.

14. STILL - A device used to distill unwanted chemicals out of liquids is called a still. Though it is known primarily for use during Prohibition, many are in use today, especially in rural areas.

15. KENNEDY – Bootlegger Joseph P. Kennedy made a fortune importing Scotch whiskey during Prohibition. His son, John Fitzgerald Kennedy, was elected President of the United States in 1960.

16. LUCIANO – Charles Luciano got the nickname Lucky for surviving a brutal beating where he was left for dead by Maranzano's men during the Castellammarese War between Sicilian gangsters.

17. BEN – Siegel, born with the first name Benjamin, was known as Ben to his friends.

20. VOLSTEAD – Though commonly believed to be the formal name of the Eighteenth Amendment, it was actually passed ten months later to authorize enforcement of Prohibition.

21. HOOVER – Appointed Director of the Bureau of Investigation in 1924, J. Edgar Hoover went on to become the first Director of the new Federal Bureau of Investigation when it was formed in 1935 and remained at that post until his death in 1972, at age 77.

22. MOONSHINE – Booze made in private stills, usually illegally and often dangerous to produce and drink, is called moonshine. The practice became widespread during Prohibition.

DOWN:

1.FLAPPER - Young women in the 1920s who wore short skirts, bobbed hair, and too much makeup; drank, smoked, treated sex casually, and generally rebelled against acceptable behavior were called flappers.

3. CICERO – Al Capone moved his headquarters to Cicero, a town on the outskirts of Chicago, to avoid Chicago police.

4. PRETTY – Amberg was so ugly he was called Pretty. Mayor Walker is said to have sworn off alcohol after seeing Pretty Amberg while drinking one night in a speakeasy during Prohibition.

5. DUTCHSCHULTZ – After refusing to shelve his plan to murder gangbuster U.S. Attorney Thomas Dewey, Schultz was gunned down on orders from Lucky Luciano.

6. REPEALED – Fourteen years after Prohibition was ushered in with the 18th Amendment, the federal government repealed it with the 21st, leaving the regulation of alcohol to the states. It is the only Amendment of the 27 to repeal a previous one.

8. GATSBY – F. Scott Fitzgerald's classic "The Great Gatsby" takes place in 1922 during the time of Prohibition.

10. CAGNEY – James Cagney starred as Eddie Bartlett in the classic 1939 Warner Brothers gangster film. The cast included Humphrey Bogart.

11. WILSON – Woodrow Wilson was President of the United States when the Eighteenth Amendment to the Constitution, or Prohibition, was ratified in 1919.

13. FDR – Roosevelt took office on March 4, 1933. The 21st Amendment, repealing Prohibition, was ratified nine months later, on December 5, 1933.

14. SPEAKEASY – Illegal bars and nightclubs during Prohibition were called speakeasies. Some, like the El Morocco and Stork Club became world renowned night spots after Prohibition ended.

18. BOOTLEGGERS – Though it technically applied to those who produced illegal alcohol, it was widely used to describe anyone who produced, imported, or distributed it during Prohibition.

19. NESS - Eliot Ness was a Prohibition agent, famous as the leader of a legendary team of law enforcement agents nicknamed the Untouchables that focused on Al Capone in Chicago

ANSWERS

MOB CROSSWORD #4:
New York Edition

ACROSS:

2. COLOMBO – Mob boss Joe Colombo was shot on stage in front of thousands at the second Italian American Civil Rights League Unity Day at Manhattan's Columbus Circle.

7. RICO - As U.S. Attorney General Robert Kennedy assigned G. Robert Blakey to investigate organized crime. Blakey later authored the R.I.C.O. Act which is widely used against organized crime figures.

8. BUCHALTER - Louis "Lepke" Buchalter co-headed Murder Incorporated with Albert Anastasia. Lepke was electrocuted at Sing Sing prison for the murder of union gadfly Joe Rosen on March 4, 1944.

11. CAPONE – Al Capone was born in Brooklyn and raised there on Navy Street off Sands Street. On a personal note, I was raised on Sands Street off Navy Street. Small world. (SG)

13. UMBERTOS - Joey Gallo and his group went to Little Italy's Umberto's Clam House after a night of partying to celebrate his 43rd birthday, where he was shot to death by Colombo loyalists.

15. VIG – Interest on shylock loans is called "vig," which is short for "vigorish."

17. LUCCHESE – Gaetano/Tommy "Three Finger Brown" Lucchese was the first boss of the New York mob family that carries his name.

18. ANASTASIA - Albert Anastasia was known as both the Mad Hatter and the Lord High Executioner of organized crime.

20. BUGANDMEYER – In their early days, Bugsy Siegel and Meyer Lansky headed up a group of young criminals known as the "Bug and Meyer Gang" or "Bugs and Meyer Gang," depending on who was talking about it.

22. VARIO – Paul Vario was a captain in the Lucchese Family who had Henry Hill as one of his men. Hill testified against Vario, who died in prison as a result.

23. BONANNO – After allegedly being kidnapped during an intra-family war, Joe Bonanno abdicated as boss of the mob family that still bears his name, and relocated in Tucson, Arizona.

DOWN:

1. COSTELLO – Frank Costello was known as the Prime Minister of organized crime for his ability to act as an acceptable go between with politicians and other officials.

3. COMMISSION - The Commission is the Supreme Court of organized crime, settling inter-family disputes and confirming leadership of various crews.

4. DONNIEBRASCO – FBI Agent Joseph Pistone worked undercover primarily with the Bonanno Crime Family using the pseudonym Donnie Brasco.

5. SOCKS – Joseph "Socks" Lanza controlled the Fulton Fish Market for the Luciano/Genovese mob family for more than three decades, and was instrumental in protecting the area's piers from sabotage during WWII.

6. GIGANTE – Genovese Family boss Vincent "Chin" Gigante used to parade up and down the street in a bathrobe.

9. LAGUARDIA – New York Mayor Fiorello LaGuardia took on the illicit slot machine business. He was famously photographed smashing the machines himself with a sledgehammer than dumping them into the water.

10. RAVENITE – John Gotti made Neil Dellacroce's Ravenite social club on Mulberry Street his Manhattan headquarters after Paul Castellano had been murdered.

11. CASTELLANO – John Gotti was convicted of having engineered the December 16, 1985 assassination of his former boss, Paul Castellano in front of Spark's Steak House.

12. PROFACI – The Gallo Brothers headed an insurrection against Joseph Profaci, the boss of what later came to be known as the Colombo Family. It lasted for a number of years with more than twenty-five killed between both sides.

14. KIDTWIST – Murder Incorporated's Abe Reles was known as Kid Twist, reportedly for his awkward walk.

16. PETROSINO – Lt. Detective Joseph Petrosino traveled to Sicily to find warrants for criminals who had escaped the island and were now operating in New York. He was murdered while there, according to legend by Don Vito Cascio Ferro.

19. MURDERINC – The group of Brownsville, Brooklyn killers under the supervision of Albert Anastasia and Lepke Buchalter were known as Murder Incorporated.

21. MULBERRY – This stretch of blocks running north/south is the main hub of Little Italy, with Italian restaurants, cafes, and souvenir shops is also the main street for the annual Feast of San Gennaro.

ANSWERS

MOB CROSSWORD #5:

Public Enemies Edition

ACROSS:

6. GURRAH – Jacob "Gurrah" Shapiro was Lepke Buchalter's partner. His nickname came from a guttural "get outta here" he'd use when irritated.

9. BABYFACENELSON – Lester Joseph Gillis, better known as "Baby Face Nelson" for his boyish looks and small stature, was a bank robber and murderer in the 1930s. He was killed in a shootout with FBI Agents in 1934 at only twenty-five years of age.

11. BOOTLEGGERS - Though it technically applied to those who produced illegal alcohol, it was widely used to describe anyone who produced, imported, or distributed it during Prohibition.

12. LEPKE – Newsman Walter Winchell arranged for fugitive Lepke Buchalter to surrender to FBI Director J. Edgar Hoover on federal charges to avoid a death penalty case with New York State. The Feds convicted him then reneged and sent him to New York, where he was convicted of murder and executed in Sing Sing's electric chair.

13. KARPIS – Alvin Karpis was a co-leader of the Barker-Karpis Gang in the 1930s. He was the last of the "Public Enemy #1" to be taken and served twenty-six years in prison.

14. PURVIS – FBI Agent Melvin Purvis led the squads that tracked and killed Baby Face Nelson, John Dillinger, and Pretty Boy Floyd. He himself was killed in either a suicide or by a gun misfiring after he'd left the FBI. He was 56 years old.

16. HOOVER - Appointed Director of the Bureau of Investigation in 1924, J. Edgar Hoover went on to become the first Director of the new Federal Bureau of Investigation when it was formed in 1935 and remained at that post until his death in 1972, at age 77.

20. ALCATRAZ – Built by the Federal Government on an island in San Francisco Bay, it was the location of a prison that housed some of the most infamous inmates, like Al Capone, from 1933 to 1963.

21. DILLINGER – On July 22, 1934 Federal Agents tried to arrest notorious bank robber John Dillinger as he left the Biograph Theater in Chicago. When he pulled a gun and tried to escape he was shot to death.

23. GETAWAY – The driver designated to transport others quickly from the scene of a crime is known as a "getaway driver." Often a second "crash car driver" follows to block authorities in pursuit of the getaway car.

24. MCGURN – Sicilian born Vincenzo Gibaldi, known as Machine Gun Jack McGurn, was an important member of Al Capone's organization believed to have planned the St. Valentine's Day Massacre. He was machine gunned to death on the seventh anniversary of the Massacre.

DOWN:

1. BOTTLES – Ralph Capone got his nickname for running bootlegging operations for his brother. He was Public Enemy #3 when Al was Public Enemy #1.

2. TOMMY - The Thompson submachine gun, or "Tommy Gun," was a weapon widely used by bank robbers and in gang warfare during and after Prohibition.

3. WARNER – In the early days of movies, some studios became known for particular genres of film, like MGM for musicals. Warner Brothers became known for turning out the best gangster films with stars like Bogart and Cagney.

4. RED – A Chicago madam, Ana Cumpănaş, who was facing deportation back to Romania as an undesirable, reported to the FBI that John Dillinger would be taking one of her prostitutes, Polly Hamilton, to movies the next day. The orange dress Hamilton wore appeared red in the marquis lights. After Dillinger's death she became known as "The Lady in Red."

5. BONNIEANDCLYDE – Bonnie Parker and Clyde Barrow were bank robbers who were well known and even glamorized during their crime spree. They were both killed by a posse of Texas and Louisiana officers in 1934. Bonnie was twenty-three and Clyde twenty-five when they died.

7. UNTOUCHABLES – The 1987 film by Brian De Palma told the story of a group of lawmen who pursued Al Capone. It starred Robert DeNiro as Capone and Kevin Costner as Eliot Ness.

8. MORAN – Bugs Moran escaped death by arriving late at his garage on February 14, 1929, when Capone gunmen dressed as police slaughtered seven of his men inside.

10. ALCAPONE – A Chicago bootlegger who had a longstanding feud with Al Capone, Joey Aiello was machine gunned to death just before relocating from the city to Mexico.

15. WARREN – Clyde Barrow was played by Warren Beatty in Arthur Penn's 1967 film, "Bonnie and Clyde."

17. BANKS – During the Great Depression banks were the prime targets of outlaws because that was where the money was in those hard times.

18. MABARKER – Kate "Ma" Barker was the mother of several criminals who ran the Barker Gang during the "public enemy era." She was killed 1935 alongside her son Fred in a shootout with FBI Agents.

19. CLYDE – The infamous Clyde Barrow partnered with his girlfriend Bonnie Parker on a crime spree in the early 1930s.

22. WANTED – Post Offices routinely had boards with "wanted posters" of criminals the FBI was hunting.

ANSWERS

MOB CROSSWORD #6:
Brooklyn Edition

ACROSS:

2. GASPIPE – The murderous Anthony Casso, who became a Lucchese underboss, then de-facto boss when Vic Amuso was arrested, then stoolpigeon inherited the nickname Gaspipe from his father, who also had mob involvement.

7. GRAVANO - At the time Gambino Family underboss Sammy The Bull agreed to testify against John Gotti, he was the highest ranking New York mobster to turn stoolpigeon.

9. MASSERIA - On April 15, 1931, Joe "The Boss" Masseria was gunned down while eating and playing cards in the Nuova Villa Tammaro restaurant in Coney Island to end the Castellammarese War between him and Salvatore Maranzano.

11. GEMINI – Fat Roy DeMeo, subject of the book "Murder Machine," maintained his headquarters at the Gemini Lounge, on Flatlands Avenue, in Brooklyn.

12. AMBERG – The signature of Brooklyn mobster Pretty Amberg was to leave the bodies of those he killed in body bags across the neighborhood.

13. RELES - Murder Incorporated turncoat Abe "Kid Twist" Reles fell or was thrown from a sixth floor window of Coney Island's Half Moon Hotel while under police protection.

14. SAHARA – Larry Gallo was strangled after being lured to a meeting, allegedly with Junior Persico, at the Sahara nightclub on Utica Avenue, in Brooklyn. He was saved from death when a patrolman entered the bar and a shootout occurred, during which the officer caught a bullet.

17. GENOVESE – After the murder of acting boss, "Tommy Ryan" Eboli, Funzi Tieri took over the reins of the Genovese Family. It is speculated that he was boss in name, while

19. CRAZYJOE – Gallo was known as Crazy Joe from the early days of his career. Believed to be responsible for the shooting of boss Joe Colombo, he was gunned down in Little Italy when he went there for seafood after celebrating his birthday at the Copacabana Club uptown.

20. WANNABES – Those men, usually young, trying to either imitate or work toward becoming mobsters are derisively referred to as "wannabes."

21. JOHNSON – Willie Boy Johnson, a close associate of John Gotti, was revealed by the government at Gotti's trial as a long time informer. He was gunned down on the street in the Georgetown development of Brooklyn.

22. MASSINO – Joe Massino was the boss of the Bonanno crime family from 1991 until 2004, when he became the first boss of one of the Five Families in New York City to turn state's evidence. Little Al D'Arco of the Lucchese Family who preceded him as a turncoat was only an acting boss.

DOWN:

1. SCARPA – In 1964, Colombo mobster Gregory Scarpa helped the FBI find three missing civil rights workers in Mississippi by torturing someone who knew where they were buried. He maintained his relationship with the Feds as a "dry snitch," feeding them information even while he rose to the rank of captain and committed multiple murders.

3. ADONIS – Joe Doto, a high ranking of the Luciano Family, later the Genovese Family, was known as Joe Adonis for his good looks and success with women, including Virginia Hill, who later became Bugsy Siegel's mistress.

4. ANASTASIA - Albert Anastasia was known as both the Mad Hatter and the Lord High Executioner of organized crime.

5. FRANKIEYALE – Brooklyn mob boss Frankie Yale sent Al Capone to work for his friend Johnny Torrio after Capone had run out his string of trouble in New York.

6. VARIO – Though Paul Sorvino successfully portrayed Lucchese captain Paul Vario as a quiet man of few words in the film "Goodfellas," he was actually quite a bit more boisterous in real life. His men's nickname for him was "Magilla Gorilla."

7. GAMBINO – Paul Castellano was designated by Carlo Gambino to succeed him as boss of the crime family that bears the latter's name.

8. CASTELLANO - John Gotti was convicted of having engineered the December 16, 1985 assassination of his former boss, Paul Castellano in front of Spark's Steak House.

10. VIG - Interest on shylock loans is called "vig," which is short for "vigorish."

15. BENSONHURST – Frank DeCicco died when his car blew up on 86th Street off 14th Avenue in Brooklyn's Bensonhurst, an area long considered significant for the number of organized crime figures that live or operate in it.

16. BROWNSVILLE - The group of mostly Jewish killers under the supervision of Albert Anastasia and Lepke Buchalter, known as Murder Incorporated, operated out of the Brownsville section of Brooklyn.

17. GOWANUS – The Gowanus Canal in South Brooklyn is infamously known among locals as a long time dumping ground for mob victims.

18. EASTERN – New York's federal courts are broken down into two districts: the Southern District, covering Manhattan and parts north, and the Eastern District, which runs from Brooklyn, through Queens, and to the end of Long Island.

ANSWERS

MOB CROSSWORD #7:
Italy Edition

ACROSS:

3. CUPOLA - The Sicilian Mafia Commission, known as Commissione or Cupola, is a body of leading Mafia members to decide on important questions concerning the actions of, and settling disputes within their organization.

5. SAVIANO - Roberto Saviano wrote the book and screenplay, "Gomorrah," about the Neapolitan organized crime organization, Camorra. For his exposing of the Neapolitan mob, a contract was put on his head that kept him in hiding for years.

6. BUSCETTA - Although he was not the first pentito (informant) in the Italian witness protection program, Tomasso Buscetta is widely recognized as the first important one breaking omertà in Italy. He was the star witness in the Maxi Trial that led to almost 350 Mafia members being sent to prison.

7. SINDONA - Michele Sindona was an Italian banker and convicted felon. Known in banking circles as "The Shark", he had clear connections to the Sicilian Mafia.

He was fatally poisoned in 1986, while serving a life sentence in prison for the murder of lawyer Giorgio Ambrosoli and threatening to tell all he knew in exchange for sentence relief.

9. UCCIARDONE - Palermo's massive nineteenth century Bourbon prison, *Ucciardone*, housed the *maxiprocesso* trial in a bunker built next to it.

10. CASCIOFERRO - Vito Cascio Ferro, regarded as the greatest Mafia don in Sicilian history, was driven out of New York by Lt. Det. Joe Petrosino in 1904. Arrested by the Iron Prefect on orders from Mussolini, Cascio Ferro's cell was treated like a shrine after his death, with only the highest Mafia members allowed to occupy it.

11. MORI - Known as the Iron Prefect, Mori was assigned to purge the Sicilian Mafia by fascist dictator Mussolini, after Il Duce had taken offense when he visited a Sicilian town with a military contingent and the Mafiosi Mayor had told him that he didn't need protection as long as he was with him. Mori performed the task with a brutal relish.

12. CAMORRA - The **Camorra** is a Mafia-type criminal organization, or secret society, originating in Italy's region of Campania and its capital, Naples.

14. PENTITI - The Italian Government passed legislation creating the judicial category *pentiti* to fight terrorism in the 1970s. In the wake of the *Maxi Trial* in

1986-87, and after the testimony of Tommaso Buscetta, the term was more often used for former members of the Sicilian Mafia who abandoned their organization and started helping in investigations.

16. ANDREOTTI – Italian Prime Minister Giulio Andreotti was investigated for his role in the 1979 murder of a journalist who had published allegations that Andreotti had links with the Mafia and with the kidnapping of Aldo Moro. A court acquitted him in 1999 after a trial that lasted three years, but he was convicted on appeal in November 2002 and sentenced to twenty-four years' imprisonment. After a number of appeals the case was thrown out on statute of limitations.

17. MAFIA - The Mafia is a criminal syndicate that emerged anywhere from 1283 to the mid-nineteenth century in Sicily, Italy, since there are no records and various theories. It is a loose association of criminal groups that share a common organizational structure and code of conduct.

19. APOLLONIA - In "The Godfather," the girl Michael Corleone marries in Sicily is Apollonia, who dies when she starts Michael's car that is rigged with explosives to kill him.

21. TOTO - Salvatore "Totò" Riina, also known as "The Beast" to his fellow Mafiosi, is a member of the Sicilian Mafia who became the most powerful member of the criminal organization in the early 1980s.

DOWN:

1. FALCONE - A prosecuting magistrate against the Sicilian Mafia, Giovanni Falcone was murdered, allegedly on orders from *Corleonese* boss Toto Riina. Falcone was on the road between Palermo and the airport when explosives were detonated under his car. His story was told in both the book "Excellent Cadavers" and the film of the same name.

2. CALVI - Roberto Calvi was an Italian banker dubbed "God's Banker" by the press because of his close association with the Holy See. Involved in one of Italy's biggest modern political scandals, Calvi was found on June 18, 1982 hanging from scaffolding beneath Blackfriars Bridge in London. His clothing was stuffed with bricks, and he was carrying around $15,000.

4. NAPLES - On January 26, 1962, Lucky Luciano died of a heart attack at Naples International Airport.

5. SACRACORONAUNITA - Sacra Corona Unita, (SCU) or *United Sacred Crown,* is a Mafia-like criminal organization from Apulia (in Italian *Puglia*) region in Southern Italy, and is especially active in the areas of Brindisi, Lecce, and Taranto.

8. RITAATRIA - Rita Atria was a witness in a major Mafia investigation in Sicily, breaking the Omertà - code of silence. She committed suicide in July 1992...a week after the Mafia killed the prosecutor Paolo Borsellino, with whom she had been working.

11. MAXIPROCESSO - The unique criminal trial of 475 alleged Sicilian Mafiosi was held in a bunker-like setting in Palermo in 1986. It ran from February 1986 to December 1987, and resulted in 360 convictions.

13. GIULIANO - Salvatore Giuliano was a Sicilian peasant, a separatist and, according to some sources a bandit who was mythologized during his life and after his death. Mario Puzo based his 1987 novel, "The Sicilian," on Giuliano's life.

14. PETROSINO - Lt. Detective Joseph Petrosino traveled to Sicily to find warrants for criminals who had escaped the island and were now operating in New York. He was murdered while there in 1909, according to legend by Don Vito Cascio Ferro.

15. NDRANGHETA - The 'Ndrangheta is a criminal organization in Italy, centered in Calabria. Despite not being as famous abroad as the Sicilian Mafia, and having been considered more rural compared to the Neapolitan Camorra and the Apulian Sacra Corona Unita, the 'Ndrangheta managed to become the most powerful crime syndicate of Italy in the late 1990s and early 2000s.

18. PIZZA - The Pizza Connection Trial, 1986, centered around a Mafia-run enterprise that distributed vast quantities of heroin and cocaine in the United States, and then laundered the cash before sending it back to the suppliers in Sicily. The U.S. defendants utilized a number of independently owned pizza parlors as fronts for narcotics sales and collections.

20. POLSI - At least since the 1950s, the chiefs of the 'Ndrangheta *locali* have met regularly near the Sanctuary of Our Lady of Polsi in the municipality of San Luca during the September Feast. These annual meetings, known as the *crimine*, have traditionally served as a forum to discuss future strategies and settle disputes.

ANSWERS

MOB CROSSWORD #8:

Atlantic City Then & Now Edition

ACROSS:

3. BOOTLEGGING - Though it technically applies to the production of illegal alcohol, it is widely used to describe the production, importation, or distribution of it, especially during Prohibition.

6. MARGARET – Kelly Macdonald plays character Nucky Thompson's mistress, Margaret Schroeder, on the HBO cable series "Boardwalk Empire."

9. JOHNSON – Enoch "Nucky" Johnson was the actual character portrayed in "Boardwalk Empire" as "Nucky Thompson."

11. CONEYISLAND – Though it represents Atlantic City, the boardwalk scenes in HBO's "Boardwalk Empire" are actually shot on Coney Island's boardwalk, in Brooklyn, NY.

13. RITZCARLTON – Nucky Johnson lived at the Ritz Carlton Hotel in Atlantic City.

15. FRANK – As Arnold Rothstein's right hand man, Frank Erickson developed the countrywide racing service with Moses Annenberg.

16. LANSKY – When Meyer's marriage to his first wife, Anne, coincided with the planned mob convention in Atlantic City, he decided to spend his honeymoon there so he could be part of the discussions going on and still show his wife a good time.

18. SAND – The boardwalk was originally built in Atlantic City to keep sand out of resort hotel lobbies.

20. BUSCEMI – Steve Buscemi plays the fictional Nucky Thompson, based on the life of the real Nucky Johnson, on the HBO series, "Boardwalk Empire."

21. RESORTS – The first hotel-casino to open in the new Atlantic City in 1978 was Resorts International. They flew nightly shuttle flights from Butler Aviation at LaGuardia Airport to Atlantic City.

23. NASCAR – During Prohibition bootleggers used small, fast vehicles modified for speed and handling to better evade authorities. They continued in certain regions like the Appalachians even after Prohibition ended, and by the 1940s were racing those cars for fun and profit, which led to the development of NASCAR.

24. SCORSESE – Martin Scorsese an executive producer of HBO's "Boardwalk Empire." He directed the first episode, which was likewise entitled "Boardwalk Empire."

DOWN:

1. CAPONE – Atlantic City hosted a meeting of young mobsters from around the country to decide what their future would be with old time Mafiosi, called "Moustache Petes" currently in charge. Al Capone represented Chicago.

2. REPUBLICAN – From the 1910s until his imprisonment in 1941, Nucky Johnson was the undisputed boss of the Republican political machine that controlled Atlantic City and the Atlantic County government.

4. KENNEDY – Bootlegger Joseph P. Kennedy, father of President John F. Kennedy, smuggled Scotch whiskey into the United States during Prohibition on the condition that the producers continue to pay his family a royalty on every bottle shipped to the U.S. after Prohibition ended, which they continue to do.

5. SYNDICATE – An understanding was agreed to at the 1929 Atlantic City Convention on a framework for a new criminal organization they called The Syndicate.

7. ROSEN - Harry "Nig" Rosen was a Philadelphia mobster who was a major organized crime figure on the east coast with influence as far as Atlantic City, Baltimore and Washington, D.C. He was especially close with Meyer Lansky and Bugsy Siegel.

8. MONOPOLY – The board game Monopoly was inspired by Atlantic City. Places like Marvin Gardens (misspelled Marven Gardens), Illinois Avenue (renamed Martin Luther King Jr. Blvd in the 1980s), and St. Charles Place (no longer exists) were all Atlantic City locations.

10. LEWISBURG – Nucky Johnson did his federal time in Lewisburg Penitentiary, in Central Pennsylvania.

12. LEPKEANDGURRAH – These two Jewish mobsters were part of the young Americanized criminals of different ethnic backgrounds who met in Atlantic City to figure out what to do about the old line Sicilians, known as Moustache Petes, in order to form the future syndicate they foresaw, where making money was more important than vendettas.

14. TAXEVASION – Unable to get Nucky Johnson on any of the crimes they believed he committed, the Feds resorted to using what they had finally convicted Al Capone of: tax evasion.

17. GOLDEN – The Roaring Twenties were known as Atlantic City's Golden Age. With the Great Depression, Atlantic City sunk to a low rent has been place until legalized casino gambling revitalized it in the late 1970s.

19. MOSES – Moses Annenberg developed the racing wire, which sent race results from various tracks around the country to bookmakers. It inspired a number of murders as mobsters fought for control of gambling after Prohibition ended.

22. SCARFO – Nicky Scarfo was sent to Atlantic City to oversee the Philadelphia mob's interests at a time when casinos were beginning to launch the new popularity and prosperity for the city. It was as much banishment from Philadelphia as opportunity in Atlantic City.

ANSWERS

MOB CROSSWORD #9:

Mob Busters Edition

ACROSS:

3. SEABURY – After promising mobster Frank Costello to go easy on the syndicate if they would support him in the Democrat Primary of 1932 against Al Smith, once elected he betrayed him and assigned former judge Samuel Seabury to hold hearings into the mob and political corruption in New York City.

5. COMMISSION - In the Mafia Commission Trial (February 25, 1985–November 19, 1986), Giuliani indicted eleven organized crime figures, including the heads of New York's so-called "Five Families", under the Racketeer Influenced and Corrupt Organizations Act (RICO)

8. KEFAUVER – The Kefauver Committee and the TV networks had agreed not to broadcast Frank Costello's face, only his hands. When asked by the committee, "What have you done for your country Mr. Costello?" the raspy-voiced Costello's reply evoked a rare laugh at the hearings: "Paid my tax!" Costello eventually walked out of the hearings.

9. TEDDYROOSEVELT – Among his many accomplishments, Teddy Roosevelt became New York City Commissioner of Police in 1895. He was later the 26th President of the United States, taking office in 1901, when President McKinley was assassinated then winning re-election to the position in 1904. He chose not to run in 1908.

12. ELIOTNESS - Eliot Ness was a Prohibition agent, famous as the leader of a legendary team of law enforcement agents nicknamed the Untouchables that focused on Al Capone in Chicago.

13. FAMILYSECRETS – In 2007 eleven Chicago Outfit members and associates, including Frank Calabrese Sr. who was testified against by both his brother and son, were convicted and sentenced to prison in what was known as the Family Secrets Trial.

16. CORRUPT – The formal name of the RICO law used by the federal government to combat organized crime is the Racketeer Influenced and Corrupt Organizations act.

18. CESAREMORI – Known as the Iron Prefect, Mori was assigned to purge the Sicilian Mafia by fascist dictator Mussolini, after Il Duce had taken offense when he visited a Sicilian town with a military contingent and the Mafiosi Mayor had told him that he didn't need protection as long as he was with him. Mori performed the task with a brutal relish.

19. UCCIARDONE - Palermo's massive nineteenth century Bourbon prison, *Ucciardone*, housed the *maxiprocesso* trial in a bunker built next to it.

20. HOOVER - Appointed Director of the Bureau of Investigation in 1924, J. Edgar Hoover went on to become the first Director of the new Federal Bureau of Investigation when it was formed in 1935 and remained at that post until his death in 1972, at age 77.

22. SOUTHERN - New York's federal courts are broken down into two districts: the Southern District, covering Manhattan and parts north, and the Eastern District, which runs from Brooklyn, through Queens, and to the end of Long Island.

23. BLAKEY – As U.S. Attorney General Robert Kennedy assigned G. Robert Blakey to investigate organized crime. Blakey later authored the R.I.C.O. Act which is widely used against organized crime figures.

24. JOEPISTONE – Undercover FBI Agent Joe Pistone infiltrated organized crime groups, primarily the Bonanno Family, as knock around guy Donnie Brasco.

DOWN:

1. MAXIPROCESSO – The unique criminal trial of 475 alleged Sicilian Mafiosi was held in a bunker-like setting in Palermo in 1986. It ran from February 1986 to December 1987, and resulted in 360 convictions.

2. PETROSINO - Lt. Detective Joseph Petrosino traveled to Sicily to find warrants for criminals who had escaped the island and were now operating in New York. He was murdered while there in 1909, according to legend by Don Vito Cascio Ferro. He is the only NY detective ever murdered overseas in the line of duty.

4. WINCHELL - Newsman Walter Winchell arranged for fugitive Lepke Buchalter to surrender to FBI Director J. Edgar Hoover on federal charges to avoid a death penalty case with New York State. The Feds convicted him then reneged and sent him to New York, where he was convicted of murder and executed in Sing Sing's electric chair.

6. EASTERN - New York's federal courts are broken down into two districts: the Southern District, covering Manhattan and parts north, and the Eastern District, which runs from Brooklyn, through Queens, and to the end of Long Island

7. FALCONE – A prosecuting magistrate against the Sicilian Mafia, Giovanni Falcone was murdered, allegedly on orders from *Corleonese* boss Toto Riina.

Falcone was on the road between Palermo and the airport when explosives were detonated under his car. His story was told in both the book "Excellent Cadavers" and the film of the same name.

10. VALACHI - In October, 1963, Joe Valachi testified publicly, on TV, before the McClellan Committee. He called organized crime, *"La Cosa Nostra,"* or "This Thing of Ours," which was a misnomer, since the term was used at the time with lower case letters to mean "this thing of ours that has no name." The world adopted the term from a semi-illiterate.

11. CASCIOFERRO – Vito Cascio Ferro, regarded as the greatest Mafia don in Sicilian history, was driven out of New York by Lt. Det. Joe Petrosino in 1904. He vowed to murder Petrosino and carried a photo of the detective with him. In 1909, Petrosino was in Sicily to gather warrants for wanted criminals who might be in New York. He was murdered there, as legend has it by Cascio Ferro himself.

14. PURVIS - FBI Agent Melvin Purvis led the squads that tracked and killed Baby Face Nelson, John Dillinger, and Pretty Boy Floyd. He himself was killed in either a suicide or by a gun misfiring after he'd left the FBI. He was 56 years old.

15. TWOGUNHART – Al Capone's brother, James, left his Brooklyn home and family at sixteen. He served in the army in WWI France and when he was discharged legally changed his name to Richard James Hart for his movie cowboy hero William S. Hart, moved to the Midwest, and became a famed Prohibition-era lawman known as "Two Gun Hart."

17. DEWEY – Crimebuster Thomas Dewey convicted Lucky Luciano on prostitution charges that many consider trumped up, using prostitutes like "Cokey Flo" as witnesses to make his case. Luciano was sentenced to 35 years in New York State prison.

21. ROBERTSTACK – From 1959 to 1963, actor Robert Stack starred as Prohibition Agent Eliot Ness in the popular ABC-TV series "The Untouchables."

ANSWERS

MOB CROSSWORD #10:

Chicago Edition

ACROSS:

6. ROSELLI – "Handsome Johnny" Roselli was an Outfit rep in L.A. and Vegas. Along with Chicago boss Momo Giancana, he agreed to try to kill Fidel Castro for the CIA. After the plots failed and an investigation was launched both he and Momo were mysteriously murdered.

8. LEFTYROSENTHAL - Frank "Lefty" Rosenthal was a professional sports bettor, former Las Vegas casino executive, and organized crime associate. The 1995 Martin Scorsese film *Casino* is based on his career in Las Vegas. Robert DeNiro starred as Rosenthal.

10. FAMILYSECRETS - In 2007 eleven Chicago Outfit members and associates, including Frank Calabrese Sr. who was testified against by both his brother and son, were convicted and sentenced to prison in what was known as the Family Secrets Trial.

11. GREASYTHUMB - Jake "Greasy Thumb" Guzik was Capone's accountant as well as the financial and legal advisor, and later political "greaser" for the Outfit.

13. COSTNER – In Brian De Palma's 1987 film, "The Untouchables," Kevin Costner played Capone nemesis Eliot Ness.

15. BUGS - George "Bugs" Moran was a Chicago Prohibition-era gangster and Capone foe during Prohibition. He missed being murdered during the St. Valentine's Day Massacre when he arrived late to meet with his men.

16. NITTI – Frank "The Enforcer" Nitti was a top henchman for Al Capone and, in fact, acted as front boss for him when heat was on. A day before he was to appear before a grand jury he went to a railroad yard where he committed suicide by shooting himself in the head.

17. GARAGE - On February 14, 1929 Capone gunmen machine gunned seven of Bugs Moran's men in a Moran garage. Fortunately for Moran, he arrived late and avoided being number eight.

19. TWOGUNHART - Al Capone's brother, James, left his Brooklyn home and family at sixteen. He served in the army in WWI France and when he was discharged legally changed his name to Richard James Hart for his movie cowboy hero William S. Hart, moved to the Midwest, and became a famed Prohibition-era lawman known as "Two Gun Hart."

21. MARSHALL – Marcello "Marshall" Caifano was a Chicago mobster who became a high-ranking member of the Outfit. He changed his name to **John Marshall** when he moved to Las Vegas.

DOWN:

1. CALABRESEJR – Made guy Nick Calabrese Jr. testified against his brother, Frank Sr., and others, including Outfit powerhouses "Joey the Clown" Lombardo and James Marcello in the Family Secrets trial in Chicago.

2. SYPHILIS - Twenty years of high living had seriously ravaged Al Capone's health. He had lost weight, and his physical and mental health had deteriorated under the effects of neurosyphilis. He eventually died of the disease.

3. COCKEYED – Louis "Cockeyed Louie" Fratto was an important Outfit mobster who was shifted over to become Des Moines, Iowa's top crime boss in about 1940, until his death. He apparently replaced Charles "Cherry Nose" Gioe, who went back to Chicago.

4. SPILOTRO – Tony "The Ant" Spilotro was sent by the Chicago Outfit to look after their interests in Las Vegas. In the movie "Casino," Spilotro and his brother Michael are beaten to death and buried in a cornfield. In the Family Secrets Trial, testimony had them really killed indoors in Illinois then buried in an Enos, Indiana cornfield.

5. OUTFIT – Unlike New York, with five mob families, Chicago has only one, which is known as The Outfit.

7. SCARFACE – Al Capone was called Scarface, especially in the movies. Howard Hawks' 1932 film of that name had Paul Muni as Tony Camonte, a hot-headed mobster with a large scar on his face.

9. THECLOWN – High-ranking Outfit member Joseph "Joey the Clown" Lombardo Sr. was convicted in the Family Secrets Trial and is currently serving a life sentence. He is alleged to either be the Consigliere or Boss of the Outfit.

11. GIANCANA – Sam "Momo" Giancana was boss of the Chicago Outfit from 1957–1966. Among his other nicknames were "Mooney," "Sam the Cigar," and "Sammy." Along with Johnny Roselli he agreed to try to kill Fidel Castro for the CIA. After the plots failed and an investigation was launched both he and Roselli were mysteriously murdered.

12. SCALISE – Partners John Scalise and Albert Anselmi were two of the Chicago Outfit's most successful hitmen in Prohibition-era Chicago. Both were arrested and charged in the St. Valentine's Day Massacre, but were released for lack of evidence.

14. TORRIO – After an attempt on his life and a short sentence for Prohibition violations, Johnny Torrio decided to leave Chicago and hand over the reins of his operations to his protégé, Al Capone.

15. BOTTLES - Ralph Capone got his nickname for running bootlegging operations for his brother. He was Public Enemy #3 when Al was Public Enemy #1.

18. ALCATRAZ - Built by the Federal Government on an island in San Francisco Bay, it was the location of a prison that housed some of the most infamous inmates, like Al Capone, from 1933 to 1963.

20. WILLIEBIOFF - William "Willie" Bioff was a Chicago organized crime figure who operated as a labor leader in the Los Angeles movie production business from the 1920s through the 1940s. During this time, Bioff extorted millions of dollars from movie studios with the threat of mass union work stoppages.

22. ACCARDO – Anthony Accardo was alternately known as "Big Tuna" or "Joe Batters." As a decades-long boss of the Chicago Outfit, Accardo moved it into new operations and territories, greatly increasing its power and wealth during his tenure.

ANSWERS

MOB CROSSWORD #11:
Bosses Edition

ACROSS:

3. ARIZONA - After allegedly being kidnapped during an intra-family war, Joe Bonanno abdicated as boss of the mob family that still bears his name, and relocated in Tucson, Arizona.

4. COSTELLO – In 1957, with Lucky Luciano and Joe Adonis both deported to Italy, Vito Genovese sent an up and coming Vincent "Chin" Gigante to assassinate acting boss Frank Costello. When Chin called out before shooting, Frank turned, which made the bullet graze his skull instead of going through it. Costello, more diplomat than warrior, decided to retire and cede leadership to Genovese instead of fighting for the position.

6. FRANKNITTI - Frank "The Enforcer" Nitti was a top henchman for Al Capone and, in fact, acted as front boss for him when heat was on. A day before he was to appear before a grand jury he went to a railroad yard committed suicide by shooting himself in the head.

10. TOMMYRYAN - Thomas "Tommy Ryan" Eboli was a New York City mobster who eventually became the acting boss of the Genovese crime family. On July 16, 1972, as Eboli sat in the parked car after leaving his girlfriend's house a gunman in a passing truck shot him five times. Hit in the head and neck, Eboli died instantly

12. PATRIARCA – Raymond Patriarca was the longtime boss of the Patriarca crime family, whose control extended throughout New England for over three decades. One of the most powerful crime bosses in the United States, Patriarca often mediated disputes between mob families outside the region.

15. JOEMASSINO - Joe Massino was the boss of the Bonanno crime family from 1991 until 2004, when he became the first boss of one of the Five Families in New York City to turn state's evidence. Little Al D'Arco of the Lucchese Family who preceded him as a turncoat was only an acting boss.

16. GAMBINO – Carlo Gambino became boss of what was known then as the Mangano Family when boss Albert Anastasia was gunned down in a Manhattan barber shop. He reigned until his death of natural causes in 1976, by which time the family had been renamed "Gambino."

18. RASTELLI – Phillip "Rusty" Rastelli was boss of the Bonnano Family from 1974 until his death from liver cancer in 1991. During his tenure he overcame challenges to his leadership by "Sonny Red" Indelicato and Carmine "Lilo" Galante by having them murdered.

19. MARCELLO - Carlos Marcello ran New Orleans organized crime for more than thirty years, and is believed by many to have been part of a conspiracy in the murder President Kennedy.

21 COCKEYED - Louis "Cockeyed Louie" Fratto was an important Outfit mobster who was shifted over to become Des Moines, Iowa's top crime boss in about 1940, until his death. He apparently replaced Charles "Cherry Nose" Gioe, who went back to Chicago.

22. ANGELOBRUNO – Known as the "Gentle Don" due to his preference for conciliation over violence, Philadelphia mob boss Angelo Bruno was shotgunned to death as he sat in his car during an internal power struggle.

23. SCARFO – Nicodemo "Little Nicky" Scarfo orchestrated a particularly ruthless regime and ordered over a dozen murders during his time as boss of the Philadelphia mob.

DOWN:

1. DAPPERDON – John Gotti was known, among other nicknames, as the Dapper Don for his impeccable wardrobe of suits, shirts, ties, and matching pocket handkerchiefs.

2. MANGANO – Vincent Mangano and his brother Phillip ran what later became known as the Gambino Family until April 19, 1951, when Vincent disappeared and Phillip was found murdered, both presumably by Albert Anastasia, who took over as boss.

4. CASTELLANO - Paul Castellano was the boss of the Gambino Family when he was gunned down by John Gotti's shooters as he left his car for a dinner meeting at Spark's Steak House.

5. LOMBARDO - High-ranking Outfit member Joseph "Joey the Clown" Lombardo Sr. was convicted in the Family Secrets Trial and is currently serving a life sentence. He is alleged to either be the Consigliere or Boss of the Outfit.

7. JOEPROFACI - The Gallo Brothers headed an insurrection against Joseph Profaci, the boss of what later came to be known as the Colombo Family. It lasted for a number of years with more than twenty-five killed between both sides.

8. GENOVESE - Genovese's rule as boss of what was then the Luciano Family resulted in the name being changed to his, which it carries to this day despite a number of bosses who succeeded him.

9. THREEFINGERBROWN - The Lucchese Family is one of the five New York mob crews, and is named for Gaetano/Tommy "Three Finger Brown" Lucchese.

11. ALCAPONE - Brooklyn mob boss Frankie Yale sent Al Capone to work for his friend Johnny Torrio after Capone had run out his string of trouble in New York. Capone took over The Outfit when Torrio retired.

13. TONYACCARDO - Anthony Accardo was alternately known as "Big Tuna" or "Joe Batters." As a decades-long boss of the Chicago Outfit, Accardo moved it into new operations and territories, greatly increasing its power and wealth during his tenure.

14. SAMTHEPLUMBER – Since his legal business front was a plumbing supply store in Kenilworth, New Jersey, Newark crime boss Simone "Sam" DeCavalcante was known as "Sam the Plumber.

17. SAMMYTHEBULL - Salvatore "Sammy the Bull" Gravano was John Gotti's underboss. He became a witness for the government after he and Gotti were arrested on murder charges.

20. GIANCANA – Chicago mob boss, "Momo" Giancana, who had reportedly worked with the CIA to kill Fidel Castro and later been part of a conspiracy to assassinate President Kennedy, was mysteriously shot to death in his basement apartment while under police surveillance.

ANSWERS

MOB CROSSWORD #12:
Tough Jews Edition

ACROSS:

3. PURPLEGANG - The Purple Gang was a mob of bootleggers and hijackers with predominantly Jewish members. They operated out of Detroit, Michigan in the 1920s.

5. REDLEVINE – A Meyer Lansky and Bugsy Siegel associate from the Lower East Side of Manhattan, Red Levine was one of the gunmen who murdered "Joe the Boss" Masseria in a Coney Island restaurant.

6. ROCKMAN – **Milton** "Mashie" **Rockman** was a Jewish mobster officially affiliated with Cleveland's Mayfield Road Mob. **Rockman** was the brother-in-law of Cleveland crime family bosses John "Johnny" Scalish and Angelo "Big Ange" Lonardo. He was involved in labor racketeering, with close ties to the Teamsters Union.

7. WEINBERG - Abraham "Bo" Weinberg was a

Russian-born, Jewish New York City mobster who became a hitman and chief lieutenant for the Prohibition-era gang boss Dutch Schultz. He disappeared in 1935, presumably murdered by Schultz.

9. PITTSBURGH - Harry "Pittsburgh Phil" Strauss was a prolific contract killer for Brownsville, Brooklyn's Murder Incorporated in the 1930s. He killed over hundred men using a variety of methods, and was executed in Sing Sing's electric chair in 1941.

12. BROWNSVILLE - The group of mostly Jewish killers under the supervision of Albert Anastasia and Lepke Buchalter, known as Murder Incorporated, operated out of the Brownsville section of Brooklyn.

13. DALITZ - A bootlegger, racketeer, casino owner and philanthropist, Moe Dalitz was one of the major figures who helped shape Las Vegas, Nevada in the 20th century. He was often referred to as "Mr. Las Vegas."

14. ROTHSTEIN - Though Rothstein is widely believed to have had his agents fix the 1919 World Series between the Chicago White Sox and Cincinnati Reds, a grand jury could find no link between him and the scandal.

16. LEFTYROSENTHAL - Frank "Lefty" Rosenthal was a professional sports bettor, former Las Vegas casino executive, and organized crime associate. The 1995 Martin Scorsese film *Casino* is based on his career in Las

Vegas. Robert DeNiro starred as Rosenthal.

19. THEGORILLABOYS – One of the names Lepke Buchalter and Gurrah Shapiro were known as was "The Gorilla Boys."

20. WAXEY – Irving "Waxey Gordon" Wexler specialized in bootlegging and illegal gambling. An associate of Arnold Rothstein, he was caught up in a power struggle following Rothstein's death. Lucky Luciano and Meyer Lansky provided the Feds with evidence that led to his imprisonment for ten years on income tax evasion.

21. CRAZYHENRY – Lepke partner Gurrah Shapiro's son, known as "Crazy Henry," had interests in men's clothing operations, was a producer on the film "Superfly," and ran gambling junkets to the Thunderbird Hotel in Las Vegas.

22. KIDTWIST - Murder Incorporated turncoat Abe "Kid Twist" Reles fell or was thrown from a sixth floor window of Coney Island's Half Moon Hotel while under police protection.

DOWN:

1. MURDERINCORPORATED - The group of Brownsville, Brooklyn killers under the supervision of Albert Anastasia and Lepke Buchalter were known as Murder Incorporated.

2. ORGEN - Jacob "Little Augie" Orgen was a New York gang leader involved in bootlegging and labor racketeering during Prohibition. On October 16, 1927, while walking on Norfolk Street in a Manhattan neighborhood on the Lower East Side, Orgen was killed by Lepke Buchalter and Gurrah Shapiro in a drive-by shooting that ascended them to leadership.

3. PHILADELPHIA - Harry "Nig" Rosen was a Philadelphia mobster who was a major organized crime figure on the east coast with influence as far as Atlantic City, Baltimore and Washington, D.C. He represented his city at the 1929 mob convention in Atlantic City.

4. AMBERG – Louis Amberg was so ugly he was called Pretty. Mayor Jimmy Walker is said to have sworn off alcohol after seeing Pretty Amberg while drinking one night in a speakeasy during Prohibition.

8. MIDNIGHTROSE - Midnight Rose was a 24 hours candy store in Brownsville, Brooklyn, where Murder Incorporated hitmen would assemble and get their assignments.

10. MEYERLANSKY - Lansky met Bugsy Siegel when they were teenagers. They became lifelong friends, as well as partners in the bootlegging trade, and together with Lucky Luciano, formed a lasting partnership

11. MICKEYCOHEN – Numerous attempts were made on the life of Meyer Lansky and Bugsy Siegel associate Mickey Cohen. Running rackets in Los Angeles, he was shot at and had part of his house destroyed by a bomb.

15. HALFMOON - Murder Incorporated turncoat Abe "Kid Twist" Reles fell or was thrown from a sixth floor window of Coney Island's Half Moon Hotel while under police protection.

17. MAXTHEJEW - Max "The Jew" Schrager was part of the Lansky group and ran a Williamsburg, Brooklyn numbers bank.

18. MOEGREENE – Alex Rocco played character Moe Green in the 1972 Academy Award winning film, "The Godfather," who got shot through his eyeglasses while on a massage table.

20. WEISS - Emanuel "Mendy" Weiss was a New York organized crime figure who worked for Brooklyn's Murder, Inc. during the 1930s. Hymie Weiss was an

Chicago mobster who became a leader of the Prohibition-era North Side Gang and a bitter rival of Al Capone.

ANSWERS

MOB CROSSWORD #14:
Film & TV Edition

ACROSS:

5. KETCHUP – One of the funniest scenes in the HBO award winning mob series, "Sopranos," is Tony Sirico stuck in a snowbound car in the woods with nothing to eat but packets of ketchup that had been left in the car from past fast food.

8. SUICIDEKINGS – Playing yet another mobster, Christopher Walken's character, crime boss Carlo Bartolucci gets his finger cut off by a group of yuppies who've kidnapped him for ransom in the 1997 film "Suicide Kings."

10. BALLFIELD – In Herb Ross's 1990 comedy, "My Blue Heaven," Steve Martin plays mobster with a heart of gold Vinnie Antonelli, who enters the Witness Protection Program and is relocated in a suburb. In the course of his adapting, he has a ballfield built for local youths.

11. CORNFIELD - In the movie "Casino," Joe Pesci's Tony Spilotro and his brother Michael are beaten to death and buried in a cornfield. In the Family Secrets Trial, testimony had them really killed indoors in Illinois then buried in an Enos, Indiana cornfield.

15. CRIMESTORY – From 1986 to 1988, former real cop Dennis Farina played Lt. Mike Torello in pursuit of Anthony Dennison's power hungry Chicago mobster character Ray Lucas, on the NBC-TV series, "Crime Story."

16. POOLROOM – In Martin Scorsese's 1973 mob classic, "Mean Streets," DeNiro, Keitel, and their crew go see Meatloaf, in a poolroom his character owns to settle a beef over money. During the discussion Meatloaf calls his adversary a "mook." While no one knows what it means, it's taken as an insult and a huge brawl ensues.

18. THUMB – In the 1984 mob comedy, "The Pope of Greenwich Village," Eric Roberts' Paulie gets his thumb cut off by Bed Bug Eddie, played by Burt Young.

19. CUCUMBER – Alec Baldwin played Frank "Cucumber" De Marco in Jonathon Demme's 1988 film, "Married to the Mob, " which also starred Michelle Pheiffer as his wife, Angela.

21. HOFFA - Jack Nicholson's portrait of Union leader Jimmy Hoffa is seen through the eyes of his friend, Bobby Ciaro (Danny DeVito). The film follows Hoffa through his countless battles with authorities and finally the mob.

22. GOTTI – Armand Assante was nominated for a Golden Globe Award for his portrayal of John Gotti in the 1996 HBO film, "Gotti."

23. BANANAS – In Roberto Benigni's 1991 comedy, "Johnny Stecchino," his protagonist's ongoing gag is that he will reach for a bunch of bananas and spirit one into his sleeve to make off with for free.

DOWN:

1. ROBERTSTACK – From 1959 to 1963, actor Robert Stack starred as Prohibition Agent Eliot Ness in the popular ABC-TV series "The Untouchables."

2. DONRICKLES – John Landis' 1992 mob-vampire (yes, mob-vampire) film, "Innocent Blood," featured Don Rickles as crime boss Robert Loggia's right hand man.

3. NOODLES – Robert DeNiro played Jewish gangster David "Noodles" Aaronson in Sergio Leone's 1984 classic mobster film, "Once Upon a Time in America."

4. CHARLIE – Harvey Keitel played the up and coming wiseguy, Charlie, in Martin Scorsese's 1973 classic mob film about wannabes in Little Italy.

6. EGGPLANT – One of the best scenes in modern film is the back and forth between Dennis Hopper who is tied up and about to be killed and his questioner, Christopher Walken, in "True Romance," where Hopper tells Walken that his Sicilian background means he's got black blood, and is an eggplant, which is *melenzana* in Italian, a term used to refer to blacks.

7. SERGIOLEONE – Leone directed the 1984 classic mobster film, "Once Upon a Time in America," starring Robert DeNiro and James Woods.

9. ALCAPONE – Al Capone has been portrayed in many films by a number of actors, including Neville Brand, Jason Robards, and Ben Gazzara. Some others are George Segal, Robert DeNiro, and to many the best of them all, Rod Steiger.

12. LUCABRASI – In "The Godfather," when the jacket of actor Lenny Montana's character, Luca Brasi is delivered wrapped around a fish, it is understood that he is dead and underwater, or "sleeping with the fishes."

13. WISEGUY – From 1987 to 1990, Ken Wahl played undercover agent Vinnie Terranova who infiltrates the mob.

14. DONFANUCCI – In "The Godfather: Part II," Robert DeNiro as a young Vito Corleone waits for the foppish and arrogant Don Fanucci outside the latter's apartment, where he shoots and kills him to cement his reputation as a "man of respect."

17. MICKEYCOHEN – Harvey Keitel gives a stellar performance as Jewish L.A. mobster Mickey Cohen in the 1991 Academy Award nominated film, "Bugsy," based on the Vegas years of mobster Bugsy Siegel.

19. CAGNEY – James Cagney played hard-nosed gangster Rocky Sullivan in the 1942 Warner Brothers classic, "Angels with Dirty Faces," which also featured Pat O'Brien, Humphrey Bogart, Ann Sheridan, and The

Bowery Boys.

20. MOBSTERS – The 1991 film, "Mobsters," stars Christian Slater as Lucky Luciano, Costas Mandylor as Frank Costello, Patrick Dempsey as Meyer Lansky, AND Richard Grieco as Bugsy Siegel.

ANSWERS

MOB CROSSWORD #15:

Mob Cities Edition

ACROSS:

1. BULGER – Informed that Christmas season arrests would be coming down, Irish Boston gang leader Whitey Bulger went on the lam from 1994 until 2011, when he was captured in Santa Monica, California.

5. QUEENS – In 1966, thirteen members of organized crime were arrested at La Stella Italian restaurant in Queens, New York. The arrests appeared on the front page of the New York Times which called the affair "Little Apalachin."

6. PHILADELPHIA – Both Angelo Bruno and Nicky Scarfo were bosses of the Philadelphia mob. Bruno, known as "The Gentle Don," was shot-gunned to death in his car in 1980. Little Nicky Scarfo is serving a life sentence for RICO charges that included drug trafficking, loan sharking, extortion and murder.

9. NEWORLEANS – On the night of October 15, 1890,

in New Orleans, Louisiana, the Chief of Police, David Hennessy, was shot down in the street. When asked who shot him before he died, Hennessy allegedly answered, "A Dago." Three hundred Italian-Americans were rounded up. Nine men were eventually tried and acquitted of the murder. A mob of thousands broke into the prison and dragged the acquitted men and two others into the streets and lynched them.

12. LONDON - Twin brothers Ronald "Ronnie" Kray and Reginald "Reggie" Kray were English gangsters who were foremost perpetrators of organized crime in London's East End during the 1950s and '60s. They were immortalized in the 1990 film, "The Krays."

15. CORLEONE – Infamous Sicilian Mafia bosses Bernardo Provenzano and Toto Riina were both from Corleone, the name borrowed from the island by Mario Puzo for his protagonist in "The Godfather."

18. HAVANA - In October 1946, Lucky Luciano secretly moved from Italy, where he'd been deported to, to Havana, Cuba. After taking a quiet route through South America, he finally arrived in Havana, where he moved into an estate in the Miramar section of the city. A mob conference took place in December at the Hotel Nacional de Cuba and lasted a little more than a week.

19. MANHATTAN - Paul Castellano was the boss of the Gambino Family when he was gunned down by John

Gotti's shooters as he left his car for a dinner meeting at Spark's Steak House, on East 46th Street, in Manhattan.

21. CICERO - Al Capone moved his headquarters to Cicero, a town on the outskirts of Chicago, to avoid Chicago police. On September 20, 1926, the North Side gang shot into Capone's entourage as he was eating lunch in the Hawthorne Hotel restaurant. Ten vehicles, using Tommyguns and shotguns riddled the outside of the Hotel and its first floor restaurant

22. CHICAGO - In 2007 eleven Chicago Outfit members and associates, including Frank Calabrese Sr. who was testified against by both his brother and son, were convicted and sentenced to prison in what was known as the Family Secrets Trial.

DOWN:

1. BRIGHTONBEACH - Russian-Jewish mobsters now dominate the Brighton Beach area of Brooklyn. Just blocks from the beach and with streets lined with Russian-owned shops, it's often referred to as "Little Odessa."

2. TUCSON - After allegedly being kidnapped during an intra-family war, Joe Bonanno abdicated as boss of the mob family that still bears his name, and relocated in Tucson, Arizona.

3. BARBARA - The Apalachin Meeting was an organized crime summit held at the home of mobster Joseph Barbara in Apalachin, New York on November 14, 1957. An estimated 100 mob members from the United States, Canada and Italy are thought to have been at this meeting, which was raided by state police. Many escaped, but more than 60 underworld bosses were detained and indicted.

4. BUFALINO - Russell A. Bufalino also known as "McGee" and "The Old Man" was the boss of the Northeastern Pennsylvania crime family, which included Scranton, from 1959 to 1989.

7. MONTREAL – The war in Montreal in the late 1970s between Sicilian and Calabrian mobsters, which drove the latter to Toronto, may have reignited as bodies dropped in Montreal during late 2012 and early 2013. The new conflict lists among its casualties, the father and son of former leader Vito Rizzuto, who returned to Montreal after a prison stint in the U.S.

8. NAPLES - Roberto Saviano wrote the book and screenplay, "Gomorrah," about the Neapolitan organized crime organization, Camorra.

10. LOSANGELES – Los Angeles' mob, known as "The Mickey Mouse Mafia," came into the public eye when its boss, "Jimmy the Weasel" Fratianno, rolled over and became a government witness.

11. SANLUCA - The chiefs of the Calabrian criminal consortium, the 'Ndrangheta, have held annual meetings, called *crimini*, at the Sanctuary of Our Lady of Polsi, in the Aspromonte Mountains near San Luca, in Calabria.

13. TORONTO - Siderno Group is the name for the seven "'Ndrangheta" clans operating in the Greater Toronto Area. The Siderno clans are part of the Commisso 'ndrina a crime family based in Calabria, Italy. The Calabrians fled Montreal for Toronto in the 1970s after losing a war for control of Montreal to Sicilian Mafiosi.

14. DETROIT - The Purple Gang was a mob of bootleggers and hijackers with predominantly Jewish members. They operated out of Detroit, Michigan in the 1920s.

16. FRATTO – Cockeyed Lou Fratto, also known as Lew Farrell, was sent by the Chicago Outfit in 1940 to replace Charles "Cherry Nose" Gioe as boss of its Des Moines, Iowa operation. He ran the Des Moines mob until his death in 1967.

17. PALERMO - Palermo's massive nineteenth century Bourbon prison, *Ucciardone*, housed the *maxiprocesso* trial in a bunker built next to it.

20.TRAFFICANTE – Santo Trafficante Sr. gained

power as a mobster in Tampa and ruled organized crime in that city from the 1930s until his death in 1954. Upon his death, Santo Trafficante Sr. gave the power to his son, Santo Trafficante, Jr.

21. CIVELLA – Nick Civella was a Kansas City, Missouri mobster who became leader of the Kansas City crime family. Civella attended the ill-fated 1957 meeting of mob bosses in Apalachin, New York. Civella's involvement with organized crime led to his being listed as one of the first entries in the Black Book, prohibiting him from entering casinos in Nevada.

ANSWERS

MOB CROSSWORD #16:

Stoolpigeons Edition

ACROSS:

2. SHELLACKHEAD – Named for his immovable hairspray hardened hair, Richard "Shellackhead" Cantarella was a New York mobster who became a captain for the Bonanno crime family and later a government witness.

4. VALACHI - Joe Valachi was the first member to testify to the existence of organized crime families. He coined the name "Cosa Nostra" in televised McClellan Committee hearings in 1963.

6. NINOGAGGI - Dominick Montiglio was the nephew of Anthony 'Nino' Gaggi, a powerful and respected captain in the Gambino family. Dominick became a government witness in 1983 after being arrested for extortion and went on to testify against his uncle Nino and the violent DeMeo crew headed by Gaggi's subordinate Roy DeMeo.

8. MIKEYSCARS – A former Gambino crime family member especially close to John Gotti Jr., Mikey Scars Leonardo is now a government informant.

11. MOBWIVES – During the taping of VH-1's "Mob Wives," Renee Graziano's ex-husband, Hector Pagan, had secretly worn a wire and taped his former father-in-law, Anthony Graziano, who was returned to prison because of it.

14. BIGPUSSY - **"Big Pussy" Bonpensiero**, played by Vincent Pastore, is a character on the HBO TV series "The Sopranos." When Tony Soprano believed him to be a rat, he lured him onto a boat, where he, Paulie, and Silvio shot Pussy, bagged him up, weighed him down, and threw him overboard.

17. CHICAGO - In 2007 eleven Chicago Outfit members and associates, including Frank Calabrese Sr. who was testified against by both his brother and son, Frank Jr., were convicted and sentenced to prison in what was known as the Family Secrets Trial.

18. GENOVESE - Vincent "Fish" Cafaro was a mobster and protegee of Anthony "Fat Tony" Salerno, a top lieutenant in the Genovese crime family until becoming a government informant and witness.

20. TUMAC - Anthony "Tumac" Accetturo is a former capo and leader of the New Jersey faction of the

Lucchese crew, known as the "Jersey Crew." Fearing that Gaspipe Casso and Vic Amuso had put a hit on him and his family, Tumac became a government witness.

21. PACIELLO - Chris Paciello is a New York mob associate and government informant who was convicted of murder. During the 1990s Paciello became a prominent night club owner in the South Beach section of Miami Beach, Florida, known for his relationships with celebrities like Madonna and Jennifer Lopez. In 2012 he took a position of nightclub promoter for the Delano Hotel, in Miami Beach, owned by another informant, Ian Schrager.

22. REYNOLD – Shortly before he began a short-term career as a government informer, Reynold Maragni was bumped up to captain in the Colombo crew. After he was discovered cheating on the Feds to make money and misusing recording equipment, they gave him the boot.

DOWN:

1. HOUSTON - Vincent "Vinny Ocean" Palermo is a former *de facto* boss of the New Jersey DeCavalcante crime family who eventually became a government witness. Living under the name "Vincent Cabella," Palermo opened strip clubs "The Penthouse Club" and the "All Stars Mens Club" in Houston, Texas.

2. SINDONA – Michele Sindona was an Italian banker and convicted felon. Known in banking circles as "The Shark", he had clear connections to the Sicilian Mafia. He was fatally poisoned in 1986, while serving a life sentence in prison for the murder of lawyer Giorgio Ambrosoli and threatening to tell all he knew in exchange for sentence relief.

3. HALFMOON - Murder Incorporated turncoat Abe "Kid Twist" Reles fell or was thrown from a sixth floor window of Coney Island's Half Moon Hotel while under police protection.

5. CHIODO – After "Richie the Wig" Pagliarulo ambushed "Fat Pete" Chiodo on orders from Lucchese boss who later turned rat, Gaspipe Casso, Chiodo hurried into the Feds' arms for protection.

7. GASPIPE - The murderous Anthony Casso, who became a Lucchese underboss, then de-facto boss when Vic Amuso was arrested, then stoolpigeon inherited the nickname Gaspipe from his father, who also had mob involvement.

9. SAMMYTHEBULL – One of the prominent figures on the TV show "Mob Wives" is Karen Gravano, whose Gambino Underboss father, "Sammy the Bull" Gravano turned stoolpigeon and testified against his boss, John Gotti.

10. GREGSCARPA - Known as "The Grim Reaper" and "The Mad Hatter", Greg Scarpa was a Colombo crime family captain and an informant for the FBI. When undergoing an operation, Scarpa got a blood transfusion from mobster Paul Mele, a body builder who was abusing steroids and had contracted the HIV virus from a dirty needle.

12. BONANNO – Joe Massino was the boss of the Bonanno crime family from 1991 until 2004, when he became the first boss of one of the Five Families in New York City to turn state's evidence.

13. SPIKE – Long time Genovese Family associate, Julius "Spike" Bernstein flipped and became an FBI informant at the age of 82, after an arrest for union corruption in 2005.

15. NATALE – Ralph Natale is a former American mobster. He was the leader of the Philadelphia crime family from 1995 until 1999, when he became the first American Mafia boss to turn state's evidence.

16. NORBYWALTERS – Michael Franzese testified against long time entertainment promoter and associate of his stepfather, legendary Colombo Family figure, John "Sonny" Franzese,

19. RIFLEMAN - Stephen Joseph "The Rifleman" Flemmi is an Italian-American mobster and close associate of Winter Hill Gang boss James J. Bulger. Beginning in 1965, Flemmi was a top echelon informant for the Federal Bureau of Investigation.

21. PATRIARCA - Vincent "Fat Vinnie" Teresa was an a Boston mobster in the Patriarca crime family who was a lieutenant of boss Raymond Patriarca, and later informed on him and entered the Witness Protection Program.

ANSWERS

MOB CROSSWORD #17:

Books Edition

ACROSS:

5. PETERMAAS – "The Valachi Papers," by Peter Maas, was released in 1972. Maas also wrote, "Underboss," the biography of Sammy the Bull Gravano twenty-five years later.

6. PACIELLO – "Mob Over Miami" is about Chris Paciello, a New York mob associate and government informant who was convicted of murder, and who, during the 1990s, became a prominent night club owner in the South Beach section of Miami Beach, Florida, known for his relationships with celebrities like Madonna and Jennifer Lopez.

7. LITTLEMAN – Robert Lacey's 1992 biography, "Little Man: Meyer Lansky and the Gangster Life," chronicles Lansky's life, discussing his boyhood with Lucky Luciano and Bugsy Siegel, his profitable associations with Frank Costello, his role as Havana casino owner, and more.

9. COSTELLO – Leonard Katz's "Uncle Frank," published in the early 70s, is a biography of Frank

Costello.

11. DEAL – Harvey Aronson's book about the rogue Campisi criminal crew of Newark, New Jersey is called, "Deal."

15. ROSELLI - One of the most significant Italian-American pop singers of his time, Jimmy Roselli was beloved by most mob guys for his moving renditions of Neapolitan songs, but despised by a few whose paths he crossed. He told his story in his autobiography, "Making the Wiseguys Weep."

16. SICILIANO – In 1970, Vincent "The Cat" Siciliano, having been put on the hit list by no less than mob boss Joseph Profaci authored his story, "Unless They Kill Me First." In it, he describes how he survived multiple attempts on his life.

17. GIANCANA - **Antoinette Giancana**, daughter of Sam "Momo" **Giancana**, the late Godfather of Chicago penned, "Mafia Princess," an autobiography in large part about her relationship with her dad.

18. BONANNO - In 1983, Joseph Bonanno wrote his autobiography "A Man of Honor," which told of organized crime's Commission. Using that information as a premise for a RICO indictment, U.S. Attorney for the Southern District of New York, Rudy Giuliani brought to trial and convicted leaders of the New York mob families.

20. TAMPA – Scott M. Deitch's 2005 book, "Cigar City Mafia: A Complete History of the Tampa Underworld" focuses on bootleggers, gambling, ringleaders, arsonists, narcotics dealers and gang murders--a variety of characters flourished in Tampa, Florida, where they battled for supremacy of the criminal underworld and Santo Trafficante won.

21. FRANZESE - Author and newspaper columnist Dary Matera, who specializes in real-life casebooks, wrote the book "Quitting the Mob" based on information provided by former mob yuppie Michael Franzese.

22. MURDERINC - Burton B. Turkus's 1951 tome, "Murder, Inc." gives insight into the mostly Jewish gang of killers that answered to Lepke Buchalter and Albert Anastasia, from his vantage point as a prosecuting Assistant District Attorney in the case.

23. WESTIES - T. J. English is an author and journalist known primarily for his non-fiction books about organized crime, criminal justice and the American underworld. His first book, "The Westies: Inside the Hell's Kitchen Irish Mob" (1990), is a best-selling account of that gang's activities.

DOWN:

1. CARLOSMARCELLO – In "Mafia Kingfish," John Davis tells Carlos Marcello's whole sinister story for the first time: from his roots in Sicily in the early 1900s, through his violent apprenticeship in the New Orleans Mafia to his reign over a $2-billion-per-year criminal empire.

2. MAFIAWIFE – After her husband, Louis Milito, a

Gambino mobster, was murdered, Lynda went on to write her story in the 2003 book, "Mafia Wife."

3. BUGSYSIEGEL – Dean Jenning's biography of Bugsy Siegel, "We Only Kill Each Other," has its title taken from a Siegel statement where he wondered why anyone cared about mobsters murdering other mobsters.

4. FALCONE – "Excellent Cadavers" is a 1995 non-fiction book by Alexander Stille about the Sicilian Mafia, concentrating on magistrate Giovanni Falcone's fight against the Mafia and his 1992 assassination.

5. PROFACI - Raymond V. Martin was Assistant Chief Inspector of the Brooklyn South Detective Squad in the early 1960's, and covered the Gallo-Profaci conflict. He recounts those experiences in his 1963 book, "Revolt in the Mafia."

8. JOEPETROSINO – Petacci's 1974 biography of the first Italian to achieve the rank of detective in the NYPD, and who was the force's point man against Mafia, Black Hand, and other criminal groups that preyed on the Italian immigrant community at the turn of the Twentieth Century, is called "Joe Petrosino."

10. GOMORRAH - Roberto Saviano wrote the book and screenplay, "Gomorrah," about the Neapolitan organized crime organization, Camorra.

12. WISEGUY – Nick Pileggi wrote the book "Wiseguy," based on information given to him by Lucchese turncoat Henry Hill. He later adapted a screenplay of it for film, under the name, "Goodfellas."

13. MIKEDASH - Welsh writer, historian and researcher

Mike Dash, who is best known for books and articles dealing with dramatic yet little-known episodes in history, penned the well researched and documented book, "The First Family," about Giuseppe Morello and the early Sicilian Mafiosi who immigrated to New York.

14. VICTORIA – The daughter of famed mob boss John Gotti, Victoria, has written a number of fiction and non-fiction books, including, "This Family of Mine: What it was Like Growing up Gotti."

19. FATROYDEMEO - Journalist and author Jerry Capeci has authored a number of mob books, including "Murder Machine," about Gambino mobster "Fat Roy" DeMeo.

ANSWERS

MOB CROSSWORD #18:

Actors Edition

ACROSS:

2. BUGSY – Harvey Keitel played L.A. mobster Mickey Cohen in the 1991 Academy Award winning film, "Bugsy," directed by Barry Levinson and starring Warren Beatty and Annette Bening.

3. CAMERONDIAZ – In Chuck Russell's 1994 comedy "The Mask," Cameron plays miserable mobster Peter Green's girlfriend who falls for the innocent Jim Carrey who is conformed into a bigger than life character when he dons a mask of a god of mischief he's found.

4. MONASTERY – In the 1940 Warner Brothers gangster-comedy, "Brother Orchid," a retired racket boss John Sarto, played by Edward G. Robinson, tries to reclaim his place while former friends try to kill him, finds solace in a monastery and reinvents himself as a pious monk.

5. BENIGNI - In Roberto Benigni's 1991 Italian comedy, "Johnny Stecchino," his stumblebum character, Dante, is a dead ringer for Sicilian mob stoolpigeon Johnny Stecchino, and is seduced by Johnny's girlfriend, Maria, to morph into the mobster so he gets killed instead of her man.

6. HOODLUM – Andy Garcia portrays Lucky Luciano in Bill Duke's 1997 film, "Hoodlum," which is set during a 1930s war for control of Harlem rackets between black and white gangsters.

7. MAX – James Woods played Jewish gangster Maximilian "Max" Bercovicz in Sergio Leone's 1984 classic mobster film, "Once Upon a Time in America."

8. PACINO - In the 1997 mob film "Donnie Brasco," Al Pacino plays the luckless Benjamin "Lefty" Ruggiero, who allows undercover FBI Agent Brasco infiltrate New York's Bonanno Crime Family.

12. CAGNEY – Best known for his MGM gangster roles, James Cagney won a Best Actor Academy Award for his 1942 song and dance performance as George M. Cohan in "Yankee Doodle Dandy."

14. CONNIE – Younger sister of director Francis Ford Coppola, Talia Shire plays troubled daughter of Vito Corleone in the 1972 Academy Award winning film, "The Godfather."

15. FRESHMAN – Marlon Brando parodies his performance as "Don Vito Corleone" in "The Godfather" as mob boss "Carmine Sabitini" in the 1990 comedy "The Freshman."

16. HOPPER - One of the best scenes in modern film is the back and forth between Dennis Hopper who is tied up and about to be killed and his questioner, Christopher Walken, in "True Romance," where Hopper tells Walken that his Sicilian background means he's an eggplant, or black. Walken laughs, gives Hopper a cigarette then shoots him to death.

17. DEVITO – In Brian De Palma's 1986 mob comedy,

"Wise Guys," Danny DeVito plays mob errand boy "Harry Valenti," who, with his partner, Joe Piscopo's "Moe Dickstein," is sent to place a $250k bet on a horse in a fixed race, but loses it when the two mistakenly place it on a loser.

18. JUSTICE – Steven Seagal stars as Det. Gino Felino in the 1991 film set in the Brooklyn underworld, "Out for Justice."

21. JAMESCAAN – In the 1999 film comedy, "Mickey Blue Eyes," James Caan plays Frank Vitale, the mobster father of Hugh Grant's fiancée, Gina Vitale, played by Jeanne Tripplehorn.

DOWN:

1. LUCABRASI - In "The Godfather," actor Lenny Montana's character, Luca Brasi is strangled at a bar while meeting with Don Corleone's nemesis, drug dealer Sollozzo. When his jacket is delivered wrapped around a fish, it is understood that he is dead and underwater, or "sleeping with the fishes."

5. BRONXTALE – Chazz Palminteri plays mob boss Sonny LoSpecchio, who mentors young wannabe gangster Calogero "C" Anello, in the Robert DeNiro directed 1993 film, "A Bronx Tale."

8. PFEIFFER – Michelle Pheiffer played Angela De Marco, wife of Alec Baldwin's character, Frank "Cucumber De Marco, in Jonathon Demme's 1988 mob comedy, "Married to the Mob."

9. FALCONE - A prosecuting magistrate against the Sicilian Mafia, Giovanni Falcone was murdered, allegedly on orders from *Corleonese* boss Toto Riina. Falcone was on the road between Palermo and the airport when explosives were detonated under his car. His story was told in the HBO film, "Excellent Cadavers," starring Chazz Palminteri as Falcone.

10. MEANSTREETS - In Martin Scorsese's 1973 mob classic, "Mean Streets," Robert DeNiro portrays the character of a character, "Johnny Boy," who is at the center of conflict among up and coming mobsters in Little Italy.

11. ALCAPONE - Al Capone has been portrayed in many films by a number of actors, including Neville Brand, Jason Robards, and Ben Gazzara. Some others are George Segal, Robert DeNiro, and to many the best of them all, Rod Steiger.

13. GOTTI – Anthony Quinn was nominated for a Golden Globe Supporting Actor Award for his portrayal of Gambino underboss Neil Dellacroce in the 1996 HBO film, "Gotti."

19. KENWAHL - From 1987 to 1990, Ken Wahl played undercover agent Vinnie Terranova who infiltrates the mob on the TV series, "Wiseguy."

20. WALNUTS – Brooklyn native Tony Sirico stole many a show as Tony Soprano's mobster underling

"Paulie Walnuts" Gaultieri.

22. MAECLARKE – In Warner Brothers' 1931 gangster film, "The Public Enemy," Mae Clarke famously gets a grapefruit squashed on her face by James Cagney's hoodlum character, "Tom Powers.

ANSWERS
MOB CROSSWORD #19:
Murders Edition

ACROSS:

1. GEMINI – Gambino soldier Fat Roy DeMeo, subject of the book "Murder Machine," maintained his headquarters at the Gemini Lounge, on Flatlands Avenue, in Brooklyn. Murder victims were lured upstairs, killed, dismembered, and later disposed of in dump sites.

3. BROOKLYN – On April 13, 1986, John Gotti's underboss, Frank DeCicco stepped into his car on 86th Street in Bensonhurst, Brooklyn. A detonated bomb planted in his car was detonated, killing him.

5. EBOLI - On July 16, 1972, acting boss of the Genovese Family, "Tommy Ryan" Eboli left his girlfriend's apartment in Crown Heights, Brooklyn around 1:00 A.M. As Eboli sat in his parked car, a gunman in a passing truck shot him five times. Hit in the head and neck, Eboli died instantly.

10. PETROSINO - Lt. Detective Joseph Petrosino traveled to Sicily to find warrants for criminals who had escaped the island and were now operating in New York. He was murdered while there in 1909, according to legend by Don Vito Cascio Ferro. He is the only American detective ever murdered overseas in the line of duty.

11. SINDONA - Michele Sindona was an Italian banker and convicted felon. Known in banking circles as "The Shark", he had clear connections to the Sicilian Mafia. He was fatally poisoned in 1986, while serving a life sentence in prison for the murder of lawyer Giorgio Ambrosoli and threatening to tell all he knew in exchange for sentence relief.

12. PALACE - After refusing to shelve his plan to murder gangbuster U.S. Attorney Thomas Dewey, Schultz was gunned down in Newark, New Jersey's Palace Chop House on orders from Lucky Luciano.

14. ABERELES - Murder Incorporated turncoat Abe "Kid Twist" Reles fell or was thrown from a sixth floor window of Coney Island's Half Moon Hotel while under police protection.

15. GARAGE - On Valentine's Day, 1929, Capone gunmen disguised as police murdered seven of Bugs Moran's men in a garage. The main target, Moran, missed the event.

18. ROSELLI – The dismembered body of Chicago-L.A. mobster Johnny Roselli, who reportedly had been part of a CIA plot to have organized crime figures kill Cuba's Fidel Castro, washed up on a Florida beach in a metal drum.

19. HABERDASHER – When Albert Anastasia saw haberdasher Arnold Schuster in a TV interview about how he'd spotted escaped convict, Willie Sutton, whom neither of them knew, he ordered Schuster killed because he said he hated stoolpigeons.

21. MARANZANO – After the young Turks like Lucky Luciano, Frank Costello, and Bugsy Siegel had eliminated one of the rival Moustache Petes who were fomenting the Castellammarese War, "Joe The Boss" Masseria, they sent a crew of killers to the remaining boss Salvatore Maranzano's office, where they shot and stabbed him to death.

DOWN:

1. GALANTE – When Carmine "Lilo" Galante, aspired to become boss of the Bonanno Family, he was murdered in the backyard of a Brooklyn restaurant, leaving his bloody body sprawled out and his last cigar stump sticking out of his death-clenched jaw.

2. MORELLO - In the 1890s, Giuseppe Morello founded a gang known as the 107th Street Mob and which would later evolve into what is known today as the Genovese crime family. Morello reportedly murdered many victims in a nearby stable, where tortured screams could be heard emanating from in the middle of the night.

4. GIANCANA - Chicago mob boss, "Momo" Giancana, who had reportedly worked with the CIA to kill Fidel Castro and later been part of a conspiracy to assassinate President Kennedy, was mysteriously shot to death in his basement apartment while under police surveillance.

6. TONYBENDER – High ranking member of the Genovese Family who had been involved in the plot to kill Frank Costello for Vito Genovese and a later plot to have Genovese imprisoned, "Tony Bender" Strollo disappeared after leaving his residence in Fort Lee, New Jersey, and is presumed to have been murdered.

7. TOLLBOOTH – James Caan, as "Sonny Corleone," in the 1972 Academy Award winning film, "The Godfather," gets machine gunned down at a toll booth.

8. CALVI - Roberto Calvi was an Italian banker dubbed "God's Banker" by the press because of his close association with the Holy See. Involved in one of Italy's biggest modern political scandals, Calvi was found on June 18, 1982 hanging from scaffolding beneath Blackfriars Bridge in London. His clothing was stuffed with bricks, and he was carrying around $15,000.

9. SPARKS - Paul Castellano was the boss of the Gambino Family when he was gunned down by John Gotti's shooters as he left his car for a dinner meeting at Spark's Steak House on East 46th Street, in Manhattan.

10. PHILADELPHIA - Angelo Bruno was boss of the

Philadelphia mob. Bruno, known as "The Gentle Don," was shot-gunned to death in his car in 1980 during an internal struggle for power.

11. SIEGEL - On the night of June 20, 1947, as Siegel sat in Virginia Hill's Beverly Hills home reading the *Los Angeles Times*, an unknown assailant fired at him through the window with a .30-caliber military M1 carbine, hitting him many times, including twice in the head.

13. ANASTASIA - On October 25, 1957, boss of what would later be called the Gambino Family, Albert Anastasia, entered the barber shop of the Park Sheraton Hotel in Manhattan. As Anastasia relaxed in the barber chair, two men with faces covered rushed in and fired at Anastasia. The gunmen continued firing until Albert Anastasia finally fell to the floor, dead.

16. BORSELLINO – Fifty-seven days after his friend and fellow anti-Mafia magistrate Giuseppe Falcone was assassinated, Paolo Borsellino was killed by a car bomb in Palermo.

17. LEPKE - Fugitive Lepke Buchalter surrendered to FBI Director J. Edgar Hoover on federal charges to avoid a death penalty case for the murder of former union activist Joe Rosen with New York State. The Feds convicted him then reneged and sent him to New York, where he was convicted of murder and executed in Sing Sing's electric chair.

20. UMBERTOS - Joey Gallo and his group went to Little Italy's Umberto's Clam House after a night of partying to celebrate his 43rd birthday, where he was shot to death by Colombo loyalists.

ANSWERS

MOB CROSSWORD #20:

Alphabet Edition

ACROSS:

2. OMERTA – The cultural attitude and code of honor rooted in Southern Italy, especially among the criminal element, that places heavy importance on a deep-rooted "code of silence," non-cooperation with authorities, and non-interference in the illegal and legal actions of others that was adopted by American organized crime.

5. EBOLI – On July 16, 1972, acting boss of the Genovese Family, "Tommy Ryan" Eboli left his girlfriend's apartment in Crown Heights, Brooklyn around 1:00 A.M. As Eboli sat in his parked car, a gunman in a passing truck shot him five times. Hit in the head and neck, Eboli died instantly.

7. WAXEY - Waxey Gordon was an American gangster who specialized in bootlegging and illegal gambling. When he was forty-three he began a relationship with twenty-year-old burlesque entertainer Gypsy Rose Lee.

8. MURDER – Also known as "The Brownsville Boys," "Murder, Inc." was the name given by the press to organized crime groups in the 1930s through the 1940s, under Albert Anastasia and Lepke Buchalter's leadership, that acted as the "enforcement arm" of organized crime.

12. SPILOTRO - In the movie "Casino," Joe Pesci's Tony Spilotro and his brother Michael are beaten to death and buried in a cornfield. In the Family Secrets Trial, testimony had them really killed indoors in Illinois then buried in an Enos, Indiana cornfield.

14. RICO - The Racketeer Influenced and Corrupt Organizations Act, commonly referred to as the RICO Act or simply RICO, is a United States federal law that provides for extended criminal penalties and a civil cause of action for acts performed as part of an ongoing criminal organization.

16. FIVEPOINTS – By the Turn of the Twentieth Century, Italians immigrants were taking over the slums that had housed Irish who had arrived a half century before, during Ireland's Potato Famine, and with it gangs. To ease the transition in the infamous Five Points Gang, leader Paolo Vaccarelli went under the name Paul Kelly.

18. COLL - Vincent "Mad Dog" Coll was a mob hitman in the 1920s and early 1930s in New York City. Coll gained notoriety for the alleged accidental killing of a young child during a mob kidnap attempt.

19. UCCIARDONE - Palermo's massive nineteenth century Bourbon prison, *Ucciardone*, housed the *maxiprocesso* trial in a bunker built next to it.

20. HAVANA - In October 1946, Lucky Luciano secretly moved from Italy, where he'd been deported to, to Havana, Cuba. After taking a quiet route through

South America, he finally arrived in Havana, where he moved into an estate in the Miramar section of the city. A mob conference took place in December at the Hotel Nacional de Cuba and lasted a little more than a week.

21. BILOTTI - Thomas Bilotti was a New York mobster with the Gambino crime family who served as underboss for two weeks. That promotion, in part, helped trigger his and Paul Castellano's assassinations in 1985.

22. KANSASCITY - Nick Civella was a Kansas City, Missouri mobster who became leader of the Kansas City crime family. Civella attended the ill-fated 1957 meeting of mob bosses in Apalachin, New York. Civella's involvement with organized crime led to his being listed as one of the first entries in the Black Book, prohibiting him from entering casinos in Nevada.

DOWN:

1. VALACHI - Joe Valachi was the first member to testify to the existence of organized crime families. He coined the name "Cosa Nostra" in televised McClellan Committee hearings in 1963, and his name became synonymous with "stoolpigeon" for decades, until mobsters "rolling over" became commonplace.

3. TORRIO – John Torrio, also known as "The Fox," was a Chicago mobster who helped build the criminal empire known as the Outfit in the 1920s that was later inherited by his protégé, Al Capone.

4. JOHNSON - Ellsworth Raymond "Bumpy" Johnson was an African-American mob boss and bookmaker in New York City's Harlem. He was the main Harlem associate of the Genovese crime family.

6. ZWILLMAN - Abner "Longie" Zwillman, known as the "Al Capone of New Jersey," was an early Prohibition gangster, founding member of the "Big Seven" Ruling Commission and a member of the National Crime Syndicate, who was also associated with Murder Incorporated.

9. DETROIT - Joseph Zerilli was a Prohibition-era Detroit gangster who led the crime family known as the Detroit Partnership from the 1930s through the 1970s.

10. PETROSINO - Lt. Detective Joseph Petrosino traveled to Sicily to find warrants for criminals who had escaped the island and were now operating in New York. He was murdered while there in 1909, according to legend by Don Vito Cascio Ferro.

11. GREASYTHUMB - Jake "Greasy Thumb" Guzik was Capone's accountant as well as the financial and legal advisor, and later political "greaser" for the Outfit.

13. ISRAEL - When Meyer Lansky was living in Israel, he fought extradition to the United States on tax evasion charges, using Israel's "Law of Return" law that applied to Jews throughout the world. Prime Minister Golda Meir backed the courts to refuse him sanctuary.

15. NEWORLEANS - On the night of October 15, 1890, in New Orleans, Louisiana, the Chief of Police, David

Hennessy, was shot down in the street. When asked who shot him before he died, Hennessy allegedly answered, "A Dago." Three hundred Italian-Americans were rounded up. Nine men were eventually tried and acquitted of the murder. A mob of thousands broke into the prison and dragged the acquitted men and two others into the streets and lynched them.

17. LANZA – "Socks" Lanza was a New York labor racketeer and a member of the Genovese crime family who controlled the Fulton Fish Market, while Mario Lanza, was an American tenor, singer, actor, and Hollywood movie star of the late 1940s and the 1950s.

23. ADONIS - Joe Doto, a high ranking of the Luciano Family, later the Genovese Family, was known as Joe Adonis for his good looks and success with women, including Virginia Hill, who later became Bugsy Siegel's mistress.

24. YAKUZA - Also known as Gokudō, Yakuza are members of traditional organized crime syndicates in Japan. They are notorious for their strict codes of conduct and very organized nature

ANSWERS

MOB CROSSWORD #21:

Alphabet Edition 2

ACROSS:

3. CASSO - The murderous Anthony Casso, who became a Lucchese underboss, then de-facto boss when Vic Amuso was arrested, then stoolpigeon inherited the nickname Gaspipe from his father, who also had mob involvement.

6. JOHNSON - Enoch "Nucky" Johnson was the actual character portrayed in "Boardwalk Empire" as "Nucky Thompson."

9. GIANCANA - Chicago mob boss, "Momo" Giancana, who had reportedly worked with the CIA to kill Fidel Castro and later been part of a conspiracy to assassinate President Kennedy, was mysteriously shot to death in his basement apartment while under police surveillance.

12. LOMBARDO - High-ranking Outfit member Joseph "Joey the Clown" Lombardo Sr. was convicted in the Family Secrets Trial and is currently serving a life sentence. He is alleged to either be the Consigliere or Boss of the Outfit.

13. NDRANGHETA - 'Ndrangheta is Calabria, Italy's organized crime syndicate. Despite not being as famous abroad as the Sicilian Mafia, and having been considered more rural compared to the Neapolitan Camorra and the Apulian Sacra Corona Unita, 'Ndrangheta managed to become the most powerful crime organization of Italy in the late 1990s and early 2000s.

14. PALERMO - The unique criminal trial of 475 alleged Sicilian Mafiosi was held in a bunker-like setting in Palermo in 1986. It ran from February 1986 to December 1987, and resulted in 360 convictions.

16. ANASTASIA - Albert Anastasia was known as both the Mad Hatter and the Lord High Executioner of organized crime.

17. JUNKETS – The mob in Vegas started gambling junkets, where they would bring high rollers to a particular casino for free flight, room, food, shows and anything else the gambler wanted as long as he kept playing. The junketeer was paid a fee by the casino. Junkets are still run to casinos today, but not with the abandon of the good old days of Vegas' mob control.

18. DEWEY - After refusing to shelve his plan to murder gangbuster U.S. Attorney Thomas Dewey, Schultz was gunned down in Newark, New Jersey's Palace Chop House on orders from Lucky Luciano.

22. ZIGANETTE – This Italian version of the card game Faro. It is usually high stakes and most often played in mob social clubs or other mob locations.

23. FLAMINGO - Bugsy named his Las Vegas hotel after his girlfriend, Virginia Hill, who was nicknamed "Flamingo" for her long legs.

DOWN:

1. WESTIES - The Westies is an Irish American gang operating from Hell's Kitchen on Manhattan's West Side. According to the NYPD Organized Crime Squad and the FBI, the Westies were responsible for 60-100 murders between 1968 and 1986.

2. MARCELLO - Carlos Marcello ran New Orleans organized crime for more than thirty years, and is believed by many to have been part of a conspiracy in the murder President Kennedy.

4. BOSTON - Informed that Christmas season arrests would be coming down, Boston gang leader Whitey Bulger left Beantown and went on the lam from 1994 until 2011, when he was captured in Santa Monica, California.

5. UNTOUCHABLES - From 1959 to 1963, actor Robert Stack starred as Prohibition Agent Eliot Ness in the popular ABC-TV series "The Untouchables."

7. OBANNION - On the morning of November 10, 1924, Frankie Yale entered rival mobster Dion O"Bannion's flower shop with gunmen John Scalise and Albert Anselmi. When O'Bannion attempted to greet Yale with a handshake, Yale clasped O'Bannion's hand in a death grip while Scalise and Anselmi fired two bullets into O'Bannion's chest and two in his throat.

8. HOWARDBEACH - Cross Bay Boulevard is the main commercial strip of Howard Beach and going northward into Ozone Park. That entire area was well known as John Gotti country, with his home in Howard Beach and his social club headquarters in Ozone Park.

10. KEFAUVER – The Kefauver Committee and the TV networks had agreed not to broadcast Frank Costello's face, only his hands. When asked by the committee, "What have you done for your country Mr. Costello?" the raspy-voiced Costello's reply evoked a rare laugh at the hearings: "Paid my tax!" Costello eventually walked out of the hearings.

11. RASTELLI - Phillip "Rusty" Rastelli was a New York mobster and former boss of the Bonanno crime family.

15. YALE - Brooklyn mob boss Frankie Yale sent Al Capone to work for his friend Johnny Torrio after Capone had run out his string of trouble in New York.

19. EASTMAN - Edward "Monk" Eastman was a New York City gangster who founded and led the Eastman Gang, which became one of the most powerful street gangs in New York City at the turn of the 19th/20th century whose greatest rival was "Paul Kelly", leader of the Five Points Gang.

20. VIG - Vigorish, or simply the vig, also known as juice, the cut or the take, is the amount charged by a bookmaker for his services. In the United States it also means the interest on a shylock's loan.

21. SINGSING - Fugitive Lepke Buchalter surrendered to FBI Director J. Edgar Hoover on federal charges to avoid a death penalty case for the murder of former union activist Joe Rosen with New York State. The Feds convicted him then reneged and sent him to New York, where he was convicted of murder and executed in Sing Sing's electric chair.

24. IACRL - Mob boss Joe Colombo formed the Italian American Civil Rights League after his son was arrested for melting down U.S. coins for the silver.

ANSWERS

MOB CROSSWORD #22:

Alphabet Edition 3

ACROSS:

5. MAGOON - Seymour "Blue Jaw" Magoon was a killer in Brownsville Brooklyn's Murder Inc gang, one of many members who were implicated by the testimony of former member and government informant Abe "Kid Twist" Reles.

9. KIDTWIST - Murder Incorporated's Abe Reles was known as Kid Twist, reportedly for his awkward walk.

10. OCTOPUS – Claire Sterling's "Octopus" is an expose of how the Sicilian Mafia uses financial influence and ruthless violence to control the international narcotics trade.

12. FALCONE - A prosecuting magistrate against the Sicilian Mafia, Giovanni Falcone was murdered, allegedly on orders from *Corleonese* boss Toto Riina. Falcone was on the road between Palermo and the airport when explosives were detonated under his car. His story was told in both the book "Excellent Cadavers" and the film of the same name.

13. ILA – Albert Anastasia's brother and Gambino mobster, "Tough Tony" Anastasia, gained control of Brooklyn Local 1814 of the International Longshoremen's Association, and eventually rose to become a vice president of the national ILA.

15. UMBERTOS - Joey Gallo and his group went to Little Italy's Umberto's Clam House after a night of partying to celebrate his 43rd birthday, where he was shot to death by Colombo loyalists.

16. WINCHELL – Newsman Walter Winchell personally had fugitive Lepke Buchalter surrender to FBI Director J. Edgar Hoover on federal charges to avoid a death penalty case for the murder of former union activist Joe Rosen with New York State. The Feds convicted him then reneged and sent him to New York, where he was convicted of murder and executed in Sing Sing's electric chair.

17. ROTHSTEIN - Arnold Rothstein, nicknamed "the Brain," was a Jewish New York racketeer, businessman and gambler who mentored a number of young mobsters who formed the new syndicate in 1931, including Meyer Lansky and Lucky Luciano.

21. DESMOINES - Cockeyed Lou Fratto, also known as Lew Farrell, was sent by the Chicago Outfit in 1940 to replace Charles "Cherry Nose" Gioe as boss of its Des

Moines, Iowa operation. He ran the Des Moines mob until his death in 1967.

22. BERNARDO - Bernardo Provenzano is a member of the Sicilian Mafia and was the head of the Corleonesi Mafia faction, and de facto capo di tutti until his arrest in 2006, after a record forty-three years on the run from authorities.

24. LUCCHESE - The Lucchese Family is one of the five New York mob crews, and is named for Gaetano/Tommy "Three Finger Brown" Lucchese.

DOWN:

1. APALACHIN - On November 14, 1957, police conducted a raid on the Upstate New York home of Joseph Barbara, during which they discovered and arrested major mob figures.

2. JIMMY - One of the most significant Italian-American pop singers of his time, Jimmy Roselli was beloved by most mob guys for his moving renditions of Neapolitan songs, but despised by a few whose paths he crossed. He told his story in his autobiography, "Making the Wiseguys Weep."

3. VINCENT - Known as "Chin," Vincent Gigante was a New York mobster who was boss of the Genovese crime family from 1981 to 2005.

4. TOTORIINA - Salvatore "Totò" Riina, also known as

"The Beast" to his fellow Mafiosi, is a member of the Sicilian Mafia who became the most powerful member of the criminal organization in the early 1980s.

6. PITTSBURGH - Harry "Pittsburgh Phil" Strauss was a prolific contract killer for Brownsville, Brooklyn's Murder Incorporated in the 1930s. He killed over hundred men using a variety of methods, and was executed in Sing Sing's electric chair in 1941.

7. GIULIANO - Salvatore Giuliano was a Sicilian peasant, a separatist and, according to some sources a bandit who was mythologized during his life and after his death. Mario Puzo based his 1987 novel, "The Sicilian," on Giuliano's life.

8. YOUNG – Actor Burt Young has played a number of mob characters in films like "Mickey Blue Eyes," "The Pope of Greenwich Village," and "Once Upon a Time in America."

11. SHAPIRO - Jacob "Gurrah" Shapiro was Lepke Buchalter's partner. His nickname came from a guttural "get outta here" he'd use when irritated.

14. CAMORRA - The **Camorra** is a Mafia-type criminal organization, or secret society, originating in Italy's region of Campania and its capital, Naples.

18. HART - Al Capone's brother, James, left his Brooklyn home and family at sixteen. He served in the army in WWI France and when he was discharged legally changed his name to Richard James Hart for his movie cowboy hero William S. Hart, moved to the Midwest, and became a famed Prohibition-era lawman known as "Two Gun Hart."

19. EXNER - Judith Exner was an American woman who claimed to be the mistress of U.S. president John F. Kennedy and mob leaders Sam Giancana and John Roselli. She was also known as Judith Campbell Exner.

20. NORMANDIE – In February 1942, a fire sunk the SS Normandie in New York Harbor. That incident resulted in the U.S. Navy asking Lucky Luciano, who was imprisoned, to help insure there would be no sabotage on the piers. Luciano sent word to Socks Lanza to protect ships docked in New York, which got him a pardon and deportation to Italy when the war ended.

23. ZELIG - "Big" Jack Zelig was one of the last leaders of the Monk Eastman Gang. Zelig was shot behind the ear and killed by "Boston Red" Davidson while riding on a 2nd Avenue trolley car.

ANSWERS

MOB CROSSWORD #23:
Colombo Family Edition

ACROSS:

4. SINATRA – When Joe Colombo formed the Italian American Civil Rights League, he reached out to Frank Sinatra to help raise money for the organization. Sinatra complied by staging a "Rat Pack" benefit concert for the League at Madison Square Garden.

5. KAHANE - In 1971, Joe Colombo aligned the Italian American Civil Rights League with Rabbi and political activist Meir Kahane's Jewish Defense League, claiming that both groups were being harassed by the federal government. Kahane appeared with Colombo on stage at the latter's First Annual Unity Day Rally at Columbus Circle.

8. SAHARA - Larry Gallo was strangled after being lured to a meeting, allegedly with Junior Persico, at the Sahara nightclub on Utica Avenue, in Brooklyn. He was saved from death when a patrolman entered the bar and a shootout occurred, during which the officer caught a bullet.

9. CANTALUPO - Joe Colombo's center of operations was Cantalupo Real Estate, on 86th Street, in Brooklyn, where he was listed as a salesman.

11. GODFATHER – Joe Colombo had a major success when he had "The Godfather" producer, Al Ruddy, drop all references to Mafia or Cosa Nostra from the film. Colombo threatened to shut down production in New York if his demand wasn't met.

12. THEGREEK - Joey Gallo and his group went to Little Italy's Umberto's Clam House after a night of partying to celebrate his 43rd birthday, where he was shot to death by Colombo loyalists. His supposed bodyguard, "Pete the Greek" Diapolos, dove for cover and caught a bullet in the ass.

13. THESHEIK – For a short time after Joe Profaci's death, "Sally the Sheik" ran the family. He died in 1963, the same year as Profaci's brother-in-law, Joe Magliocco.

15. CHURCH – Mob boss, Joe Profaci was a devout Catholic who made generous cash donations to Catholic charities. In May 1952, a thief stole valuable jeweled crowns from the Regina Pacis Votive shrine in Brooklyn. Profaci sent his men to recover the crowns and reportedly kill the thief, which they did.

16. JOEJELLY – Mario Puzo formed a number of his incidents in "The Godfather" based on real activities during the Gallo-Profaci War. "Joe Jelly" was one of the most feared killers in the Gallo crew. One day a car drove by Gallo headquarters and a fish wrapped in what was instantly recognized as Joe Jelly's jacket told the Gallos they'd lost Jelly to the sea.

18. FRANKIESHOTS – The murder of "Frankie Shots" Abbatamarco on Joe Profaci's orders, because of a money issue, launched a rebellion within his family known as the Gallo-Profaci War

19. GAMBINO - Joe Magliocco, also called "The Fat Man," took over the Profaci family when his brother-in-law, Joe Profaci died of cancer. When Joe Bonanno convinced him to join in a plot to kill Carlo Gambino and other bosses, Magliocco gave orders to handle it to Joe Colombo, who promptly informed Gambino of the conspiracy. The Fat Man's heart gave out that same year.

20. RATS – Colombo killer "Big Dino" Calabro bought himself a mere three year sentence by testifying against others, including his cousin, "Little Dino" Saracino. Frank Sparaco was to testify against one of Junior Persico's sons, but a guilty plea kept him off the stand.

21. UMBERTOS - Joey Gallo and his group went to Little Italy's Umberto's Clam House after a night of partying to celebrate his 43rd birthday, where he was shot to death by Colombo loyalists.

22. MARTIN - Raymond V. Martin was Assistant Chief Inspector of the Brooklyn South Detective Squad in the early 1960's, and covered the Gallo-Profaci conflict. He recounts those experiences in his 1963 book, "Revolt in the Mafia."

23. CHICAGO – Joe Profaci operated a grocery and bakery in Chicago when he first arrived from Italy. He later relocated to Brooklyn, New York, where he became boss of one of the five families in that city, which later would become known as the Colombo Family.

DOWN:

1. COLUMBUSCIRCLE – Joe Colombo held his first and second Italian American Civil Rights League Unity Days at Columbus Circle in Manhattan. He got shot in front of thousands at the second rally.

2. OLIVEOIL – Joseph Profaci maintained an olive oil import business, known as Mama Mia Importing Company, leading to his nickname as "Olive Oil King."

3. LUNA – "Crazy Joe" Gallo went to prison for

extortion when he threatened a business owner with a hospital stay, while detectives the businessman, Teddy Moss, had contacted were sitting nearby and heard the threats.

6. ALKASELTZER – Colombo found offensive an Alka Seltzer TV commercial, which had a guy sitting on his bed in the middle of the night suffering from a "spicy meatball." To Joe, it looked like they were poking fun at Italians. At the height of his League power, he pressured Alka Seltzer to pull the ad from the air.

7. APPLES – Hugh "Apples" Macintosh was a Persico gunman who got shot by Gallo men during the Gallo-Profaci War.

10. THESIDGE – During the first Gallo-Profaci war, Profaci's Consigliere Charles "the Sidge" LoCicero negotiated with the Gallos and all the hostages they had taken for leverage were released peacefully

14. SCARPA - In 1964, Colombo mobster Gregory Scarpa helped the FBI find three missing civil rights workers in Mississippi by torturing someone who knew where they were buried. He maintained his relationship with the Feds as a "dry snitch," feeding them information even while he rose to the rank of captain and committed multiple murders.

16. JOHNSON – A black hustler named Jerome Johnson, posing as a photojournalist, came up behind Joe Colombo as he prepared to speak at the second annual Unity Day Rally and shot him in the head. Johnson was killed instantly by Colombo bodyguards.

17. LUPARELLI - Unknown to Joe Gallo, Colombo associate Joseph Luparelli was sitting at the bar when Joe Gallo's party entered Umberto's. Luparelli hurried to another restaurant that was a Colombo hangout. After the Colombo men had armed and gone to Umberto's, where they killed Gallo, Luparelli got scared that as a witness he'd be killed too and became an informer on the events for protection.

ANSWERS

MOB CROSSWORD #24:

Lucchese Family Edition

ACROSS:

2. TRAMUNTI - In 1967, with the death of Lucchese boss Tommy Lucchese, Carmine "Mr. Gribbs" Tramunti, became the official boss of the Lucchese family

5. GASPIPE - The murderous Anthony Casso, who became a Lucchese underboss, then de-facto boss when Vic Amuso was arrested, then stoolpigeon inherited the nickname Gaspipe from his father, who also had mob involvement.

9. PROFACI - In early 1961 the Gallo crew attempted to kidnap the entire Profaci leadership. Profaci escaped capture, but after having their release negotiated, exacted revenge that launched a years-long war. Tommy Lucchese backed the Gallos from the early days on.

12. TONYDUCKS - Antonio "Tony Ducks" Corallo was a New York City mobster and boss of the Lucchese crime family from the 1970s to the 1980s.. Corallo exercised a tremendous control over trucking and construction unions in New York.

14. LEWISBURG - Giovanni "Johnny Dio" Dioguardi was an organized crime figure and a labor racketeer in the Lucchese Family. His last years were spent incarcerated at Lewisburg Federal Penitentiary.

15. LITTLEAL - – Little Al D'Arco is a New York mobster who became the acting boss of Lucchese crime family. He was the first boss, acting or otherwise, of a New York crime family to become a government witness.

16. COMMISSION - The Commission is the Supreme Court of organized crime, settling inter-family disputes and confirming leadership of various crews, including Lucchese, originally represented by Tommy Gagliano then its namesake, Tommy "Three Finger Brown" Lucchese.

18. THREEFINGERBROWN - Lucchese worked in a machine shop until 1915, when an industrial accident amputated his right thumb and forefinger, accounting for his nickname of "Three Finger Brown."

19. FRENCHCONNECTION - Carmine "Mr. Gribbs" Tramunti was a New York mobster who was the boss of the Lucchese crime family. Tramunti helped build the massive French Connection heroin smuggling ring.

22. PILEGGI - Nick Pileggi wrote the book "Wiseguy," based on information given to him by Lucchese turncoat Henry Hill. He later adapted a screenplay of it for film, under the name, "Goodfellas."

23. GANGBUSTERS – Ernest Volksman's "Gangbusters: The Destruction of America's Last Great Mafia Dynasty" is journalistic account of the rise and fall of the Lucchese Family and how it was left in shambles in the course of internal conflict and relentless law-enforcement assaults

25. MARCUS – In 1967, Tony Ducks was indicted on charges of receiving a kickback payment from a contractor for the renovation of the Jerome Park Reservoir in the Bronx. Also indicted was James L. Marcus, the former city water commissioner.

DOWN:

1. IDLEWILD - Dedicated as New York International Airport in 1948, the airport was more commonly known as **Idlewild Airport** until 1963, when it was renamed after John F. Kennedy, where the famed Lucchese robbery of Lufthansa Airlines took place.

3. AMUSO - Vittorio "Little Vic" Amuso is a New York

mobster and was Boss of the Lucchese crime family from 1987 to 2012. He became boss when he and Gaspipe Casso were told by "Christy Tick" to decide who would be boss and who would be underboss when he and underboss, "Tom Mix," went to prison. They decided Casso would be underboss for Amuso.

4. WISEGUY - Nick Pileggi wrote the book "Wiseguy," based on information given to him by Lucchese turncoat Henry Hill. It later was adapted for film under the name, "Goodfellas."

6. CHIODO – When "Richie the Wig" Pagliarulo ambushed "Fat Pete" Chiodo on orders from Lucchese boss who later turned rat, Gaspipe Casso, the bullets failed to pass through Chiodo's girth and hit vital organs. hurried into the Feds' arms for protection.

7. VARIO – In Scorsese's "Goodfellas," Paul Sorvino played "Paul Cicero," the Lucchese captain based on real life Canarsie based mobster, Paul Vario.

8. JAGUAR - For four months a bug in Tony Ducks' Jaguar transmitted mob conversations between him and his driver, Sal Avellino, to agents trailing discreetly in various "chase cars," which rebroadcast the signals to a recording van and were used in the Commission Case.

10. RIESEL – In 1956, journalist Victor Riesel was subject to an attack in which sulphuric acid was thrown in his face as he was leaving Lindy's, a famous restaurant in Manhattan. Riesel had been reporting on union corruption. A few months later, Lucchese mobster Johnny Dio was arrested for conspiracy in the attack. Charges were dropped for lack of evidence.

11. AVELLINO - For four months a bug in Tony Ducks' Jaguar transmitted intimate mob conversations between "Tony Ducks" Corallo and his driver, Sal Avellino.

13. TEAMSTERS – Tommy Lucchese wielded a lot of strength in New York's garment center, where he had various financial interests. Part of that strength came from the intimate working relationship he had with the Teamsters Union.

17. JOEPESCI - In the 1995 Academy Award winning film, "Goodfellas," Joe Pesci portrays whackadoodle Lucchese murderer Tommy DeSimone.

20. CANCER - On July 13, 1967, Tommy Lucchese died of a malignant brain tumor at his home in the Lido Beach area of Long Island.

21. IMPELLITTERI - Lucchese became one of the most well-respected Cosa Nostra bosses of the Post-WWII era. He maintained close relationships with New York City politicians, including Mayor Vincent Impellitteri.

24. BURKE – The character Robert DeNiro portrayed in the movie, "Goodfellas," Jimmy Conway, is closely based on Lucchese mobster, "Jimmy the Gent" Burke.

ANSWERS

MOB CROSSWORD #26:

Genovese Family Edition

ACROSS:

2. MORETTI - By the early 1940s, Frank Sinatra had achieved national popularity and wanted a more lucrative recording contract, but Tommy Dorsey refused to release him. Sinatra called Genovese underboss Willie Moretti for help. In a meeting with Dorsey, Moretti jammed a gun barrel down his throat and threatened to kill Dorsey if he did not release Sinatra. Dorsey sold the contract to Sinatra for one dollar.

3. TOMMYRYAN - On July 16, 1972, acting boss of the Genovese Family, "Tommy Ryan" Eboli left his girlfriend's apartment in Crown Heights, Brooklyn around 1:00 A.M. As Eboli sat in his parked car, a gunman in a passing truck shot him five times. Hit in the head and neck, Eboli died instantly.

5. COPPOLA - Michael "Trigger Mike" Coppola was a

New York mobster who became a captain of the 116th Street Crew branch of the Genovese crime family. Coppola headed many Genovese family operations from the late 1930s until the early 1960s

7. BLUEEYES - Vincent "Jimmy Blue Eyes" Alo was a New York mobster and member of the Genovese crime family who set up casino operations with mob associate Meyer Lansky in Florida and Cuba.

8. EASTHARLEM - In the 1890s, Giuseppe Morello founded a gang in East Harlem known as the 107th Street Mob, and which would later evolve into what is known today as the Genovese crime family.

10. NAPLES - Lucky Luciano helped the U.S. Army invade Sicily by sending word to the island to welcome them. He was released from prison early and deported to Naples, Italy as a result of his aid.

12. NORMANDIE - In February 1942, a fire sunk the SS Normandie in New York Harbor. That incident resulted in the U.S. Navy asking Lucky Luciano, who was imprisoned, to help insure there would be no sabotage on the piers. Luciano sent word to Socks Lanza to protect ships docked in New York, which got him a pardon and deportation to Italy when the war ended.

14. ANNA – In 1931, Genovese's first wife died of tuberculosis and he quickly announced his intention to marry Anna Petrillo, who was already married to Gerard Vernotico, who was coincidentally tossed from a roof to his death, clearing the way for Vito and Anna to wed.

16. DEWEY - After refusing to shelve his plan to murder gangbuster U.S. Attorney Thomas Dewey, Schultz was gunned down in Newark, New Jersey's Palace Chop House on orders from Lucky Luciano.

18. COKIEFLO - Crimebuster Thomas Dewey convicted Lucky Luciano on prostitution charges that many consider trumped up, using prostitutes like "Cokey Flo" as witnesses to make his case. Luciano was sentenced to 35 years in New York State prison.

20. VALACHI - After Joe Valachi beat an inmate to death in Lewisburg Penitentiary who he mistakenly thought Vito Genovese had sent to kill him, he turned to the Feds for help and became an informer.

22. TRIANGLE – Chin Gigante's crew was based at the Triangle Social Club at 208 Sullivan Street, but also met at the Dante Social Club at 81 McDougal Street and the Panel Social Club at 208 Thompson Street, all in Greenwich Village, New York.

24. VINCENT - Known as "Chin," Vincent Gigante was a New York mobster who was boss of the Genovese crime family from 1981 to 2005.

DOWN:

1. FRANKCOSTELLO - In a failed murder attempt ordered by Vito Genovese in 1957, future mob boss Vincent "Chin" Gigante shot acting boss of the family Frank Costello. The murder failed when Chin called to Costello as he fired and the latter turned his head, making the bullet graze his skull instead of killing him.

4. FORTLEE - High ranking member of the Genovese Family who had been involved in the plot to kill Frank Costello for Vito Genovese and a later plot to have Genovese imprisoned, "Tony Bender" Strollo disappeared after leaving his residence in Fort Lee, New Jersey, and is presumed to have been murdered.

6. SOCKSLANZA - Joseph "Socks" Lanza controlled the Fulton Fish Market for the Luciano/Genovese mob family for more than three decades, and was instrumental in protecting the area's piers from sabotage during WWII.

9. JAKE – Meyer Lansky's brother, Jake, brought Waxey Gordon's financial records to the Feds in order to take him off the street to avoid a war, called "War of the

Jews" at the time, between him and close Lansky associate Longy Zwillman, of New Jersey.

11. BATHROBE – Vincent "Chin" Gigante was known to be paraded up and down Sullivan Street, where his Greenwich Village social club was, in a bathrobe, acting as though he was playing with less than a full deck.

13. MASSERIA - On April 15, 1931, Joe "The Boss" Masseria was gunned down in the Nuova Villa Tammaro restaurant in Coney Island while his underling, Lucky Luciano, conveniently went to the men's room, to end the Castellammarese War between him and Salvatore Maranzano.

15. BOCCIA - Ferdinand "The Shadow" Boccia was a New York mobster and gambling racketeer who was killed by Vito Genovese, who would flee the United States to Italy to avoid prosecution.

17. CARLOTRESCA - Carlo Tresca was an Italian-born American newspaper editor, orator, and labor organizer who was a leader of the Industrial Workers of the World during the decade of the 1910s and a vocal critic of Mussolini and the Mafia. Conflicting reports have him killed on orders from Genovese as a favor to Il Duce or by Lilo Galante as a favor to Frank Costello's pal, political broker Generoso Pope or on orders from the

Bonanno underboss, Frank Garofalo.

19. FATTONY - Anthony "Fat Tony" Salerno was a New York mobster who served as front boss of the Genovese crime family to family boss Vincent "The Chin" Gigante from the 1970s until his conviction in 1986 on the Commission Case.

21. AIRPORT - On January 26, 1962, Lucky Luciano died of a heart attack at Naples International Airport.

23. BETILLO - Crimebuster Thomas Dewey convicted Lucky Luciano and "Little Davey" Betillo on prostitution charges that many consider trumped up, using prostitutes like "Cokey Flo" as witnesses to make his case. Luciano was sentenced to 35 years in New York State prison.

ANSWERS

MOB CROSSWORD #26:

Roaring Twenties Edition

ACROSS:

1. ROTHSTEIN - On November 4, 1928, mob gambler and financierArnold Rothstein was shot and mortally wounded during a business meeting at Manhattan's Park Central Hotel at Seventh Avenue near 55th Street

3. MARANZANO – When Don Vito Cascio Ferro decided to make a bid for control of Mafia operations in the United States from his base in Castellammare del Golfo, he sent Salvatore Maranzano to the U.S. to seize control of the Castellammarese faction that included Joseph "Joe Bananas" Bonanno, Stefano Magaddino, Joseph Profaci, and Joe Aiello.

7. FULTON - Born in Palermo, Sicily, Joseph "Socks" Lanza immigrated to the United States and settled in New York working as a handler in Lower Manhattan's Fulton Fish Market. Lanza soon became involved in labor union activity and, by 1923, had become an organizer for the

United Seafood Workers union (USW).

14. ACCARDO - Anthony Accardo was alternately known as "Big Tuna" or "Joe Batters." As a decades-long boss of the Chicago Outfit, Accardo moved it into new operations and territories, greatly increasing its power and wealth during his tenure.

15. LEPKEANDGURRAH - On October 16, 1927, while walking on Norfolk Street on the Lower East Side of Manhattan, gang boss "Little Augie" Orgen was killed by Lepke Buchalter and Gurrah Shapiro in a drive-by shooting, which allowed the two to take over leadership of the gang.

17. PORELLO - Rick Porrello was a Cleveland-area police chief and author of "The Rise and Fall of the Cleveland Mafia." He began writing his first book during research into the murders of his grandfather and three uncles, who were Cleveland mob leaders killed in Prohibition-era violence.

18. LEGS - Jack "Legs" Diamond was an Irish-American gangster in Philadelphia and New York City during the Prohibition era. A bootlegger and close associate of Arnold Rothstein, Diamond escaped a number of attempts on his life between 1916 and 1931, earning him the nickname, "Legs."

19. SPEAKEASY - Illegal bars and nightclubs during Prohibition were called speakeasies. Some, like the El

Morocco and Stork Club became world renowned night spots after Prohibition ended.

20. SCALISE - Partners John Scalise and Albert Anselmi were two of the Chicago Outfit's most successful hitmen in Prohibition-era Chicago. Both were arrested and charged in the St. Valentine's Day Massacre, but were released for lack of evidence.

21. HARLEM - Stephanie St. Clair was a female gang leader who ran numerous criminal enterprises in Harlem, New York in the early part of the 20th century. After the end of Prohibition syndicate mobsters saw a decrease in profits and decided to move in on the Harlem gambling scene. Dutch Schultz was the first to move in.

22. ATLANTICCITY – The Atlantic City mob conference was a historic summit of leaders of organized crime in the United States that had a major impact on the future direction of the criminal underworld. It was also the first concrete move toward a National Crime Syndicate.

23. HAWTHORNE - Al Capone moved his headquarters to Cicero, a town on the outskirts of Chicago, to avoid Chicago police. On September 20, 1926, the North Side gang shot into Capone's entourage as he was eating lunch in the Hawthorne Hotel restaurant. Ten vehicles, using Tommyguns and shotguns riddled the outside of the Hotel and its first floor restaurant.

DOWN:

2. THEOUTFIT - The Chicago Outfit, also known as the Chicago Syndicate, Chicago Mafia, Chicago Mob, or simply the Outfit, is a crime syndicate based in Chicago, Illinois, USA.

4. OWNEYMADDEN - Owney "The Killer" Madden was a leading underworld figure in Manhattan, most notable for his involvement in organized crime during Prohibition. He also ran the famous Cotton Club and was a leading boxing promoter in the 1930s

5. ELMOROCCO - In 1931, John Perona, an Italian immigrant, opened El Morocco as a speakeasy at 154 East 54th Street between Lexington Avenue and Third Avenue, where the Citigroup Center now stands. After prohibition was repealed, it became one of the most popular establishments in New York City due to its regular clientele of fashionable society, politicians, and entertainers.

6. BOOTLEGGERS - Though it technically applied to those who produced illegal alcohol, it was widely used to describe anyone who produced, imported, or distributed it during Prohibition.

8. BOGART - The Roaring Twenties is a 1939 Warner Brothers crime thriller starring James Cagney, Priscilla Lane, Humphrey Bogart and Gladys George.

9. PROHIBITION - The National Prohibition Act, known informally as the Volstead Act, was enacted to carry out the intent of the Eighteenth Amendment, which established prohibition in the United States.

10. BUGSMORAN - George "Bugs" Moran was a Chicago Prohibition-era gangster and Capone foe during Prohibition. He missed being murdered during the St. Valentine's Day Massacre when he arrived late to meet with his men.

11. FRANKIEYALE - Brooklyn mob boss Frankie Yale sent Al Capone to work for his friend Johnny Torrio after Capone had run out his string of trouble in New York.

12. KENNEDY - Bootlegger Joseph P. Kennedy made a fortune importing Scotch whiskey during Prohibition. His son, John Fitzgerald Kennedy, was elected President of the United States in 1960.

13. MUSSOLINI - To gain control of the South, especially Sicily, Mussolini appointed Cesare Mori as a Prefect of the city of Palermo, with the charge of eradicating the Mafia at any price. In 1926, Cascio Ferro was arrested in a big Mafia round-up in an area that included Corleone and Bisacquino.

16. RACINGWIRE - Several sources have documented publisher Moses Annenberg's links to organized crime, such as his ownership of the National Racing Wire, though it has always been widely under reported.

20. SCARFACE - Al Capone was called Scarface, especially in the movies. Howard Hawks' 1932 film of that name had Paul Muni as Tony Camonte, a hot-headed mobster with a large scar on his face.

Also by Sonny Girard:

Sonny Girard's Mob Reader

Sonny Girard's Mob Reader is the ultimate organized crime primer from someone who's actually spent his entire life as an insider and writes without confessions. Unlike mob turncoats (i.e.: rats) he writes authentically without self-serving, gratuitous excuses. His old friends, whoever's left, are still his best friends. Mob Reader contains his original articles, short snapshots of mostly unknown characters, reviews of his favorite mob books, letters from visitors to www.SonnysMobCafe.com, and sample pages of his previously published novels.

"SEX AND ROMANCE, MOBSTERS AND SPIES. WHAT MORE COULD A GIRL ASK FOR?"

- Kim Delaney, actor, "NYPD Blue" (ABC-TV)

"Mob Reader captures the heart of the mob life without glorifying it or attacking it; just tells it like it is."

- Jennifer Graziano, Creator and Executive Producer of "Mob Wives" franchise, VH-1

"Sonny Girard's Mob Reader takes you on a journey into the real mob: how they killed, intriguing, suspenseful, with an insider's view of life in the mob"

- Tony "Nap" Napoli, best selling author of *My Father My Don*

"Nobody knows the inside outs of mob life better than Sonny. No bullshit; no lies. Sonny Girard's Mob Reader is great reading."

- Frank DiMatteo, Publisher, Mob Candy Magazine

Also by Sonny Girard:

BLOOD OF OUR FATHERS

"An authentic thriller from a mob guy who's obviously been there."

-- **Nicholas Pileggi, Author of** *Wiseguy (Film name: Goodfellas)*

With razor-sharp honesty, Sonny Girard, an ex-mobster himself, tells the story of "Mickey Boy" Messina, just paroled from prison for a crime he didn't commit, and in love with his brother's ex-girlfriend, Laurel, a complication on his road to becoming a "made man" in the Calabra Crime Family. Mickey Boy's mother, Connie, carries a secret of an affair that could cost her son his life. Chrissy Augusta, a top mobster's teenage daughter, walks a dangerous tightrope with a secret lover from another *Cosa Nostra* family. All three affairs collide with tragic results in the midst of a bloody mob war.

From Little Italy social clubs to mob bedrooms, BLOOD OF OUR FATHERS is a tale of intimacy, loyalty and betrayal in the underworld – an underworld caught up in a war that threatens the life of everyone associated with it. Three love stories in a mob setting rather than a mob story, BLOOD OF OUR FATHER portrays family secrets, authentic organized crime politics, and bloodshed that crackles with vivid detail.

"Girard shines as a storyteller...(he has an) authoritative grasp of the Mafia's inner workings."

-- Publishers Weekly

"This story is not just for guys. It's like Jackie Collins meets Mario Puzo. I loved it."

--Katherine Narducci, Actor (Sopranos, Bronx Tale, etc.)

"Sonny Girard captures the heart of the mob life without glorifying it or attacking it; just tells it like it is."

- Jennifer Graziano, Creator and Executive Producer of "Mob Wives" franchise, VH-1

Also by Sonny Girard:

SINS OF OUR SONS

Not since Mario Puzo's Godfather *has a novel so passionately captured the soul of organized crime as did mob insider Sonny Girard's astounding debut,* Blood of Our Fathers. *Now Girard brings us the extraordinary successor, an explosive drama of the changes rocking the American Mafia...*

In one swift stroke, an assassin's bullet elevated Mickey Boy Messina from foot soldier to boss of the Calabra Crime Family – and left him with a legacy of pain and confusion. Now Mickey Boy is walking a delicate line, caught between the thrill of a power he never dreamed would be his, and Frank Halloran, a rock-hard parole officer determined to bring him down; between Don Peppino Palermo, a treacherous old Sicilian boss scheming to change the face of New York's organized crime, and Laurel, Mickey Boy's smart, sexy, no-nonsense wife. For her sake – and for the sake of Hope, the baby daughter he prayed for to end his line of mob inheritance – Mickey Boy is filled with a new ambition: to lead his people away from their criminal tradition and into the legitimate world. But in a dark society laced with misplaced trusts, and peppered with sudden and violent revenge, the road into daylight has always been paved with blood and sorrow…

"Sonny Girard…takes you on a journey into the real mob: how they killed, intriguing, suspenseful, with an insider's view of life in the mob"

- Tony "Nap" Napoli, author of "My Father, My Don"

"Nobody knows the inside outs of mob life better than Sonny. No bullshit; no lies."

- Frank DiMatteo, Publisher, Mob Candy Magazine

[Sonny Girard is] *"…A man who knows the world of crime."*

-- **Bill O'Reilly,** *The O'Reilly Factor, Fox News Channel*

Also by Sonny Girard:

SNAKE EYES

Small-time mobster Neil DiChristo is a happy-go-lucky bookmaker who prefers wine, women, and good food, not necessarily in that order, to any serious work or crime. One morning he is dragged out of his house by a team of FBI agents who have put together enough false information to throw him in prison for life and mark him as an informant to get him killed. All they want, they say, is for him to get close enough to a Russian operative to bring him down. It seems the only chink is the Russian's gambling habit, and DiChristo's credentials in that area give him the greatest chance of gaining the supposed spy's confidence. With no good option available, he reluctantly agrees.

From the opening page, Neil DiChristo is catapulted into a bizarre world of intrigue, murder, and more sex and romance than is healthy for anyone—where nothing is as it seems and his fate is beyond his control. All Neil wants is to be left alone.

Fat chance.

"Girard shines as a storyteller."

—**Publisher's Weekly**

"Sex and romance, mobsters and spies. What more could a girl ask for?"

—**Kim Delaney, Actor (*NYPD Blue* – ABC TV).**

"Sonny certainly knows all the players, and when it comes to this kind of book he's as good as anyone."

—**James Caan, Actor (*Godfather, Vegas*/NBC-TV, etc.)**

"Girard captivates the reader. He is an accomplished storyteller."

—**Literary Journal**

FOR MORE MOB STUFF, INCLUDING BLOGS, MOLLS, MOB JOKES, TO BUY AUTOGRAPHED COPIES OF SONNY GIRARD BOOKS, AND TO CONTACT HIM WITH QUESTIONS OR COMMENTS, VISIT:

www.SonnysMobCafe.com

**WE LOOK FORWARD TO
HEARING FROM YOU.
ON OUR GRILL SONNY PAGE
AT
WWW.SONNYSMOBCAFE.COM**

Thank You

9 780982 169674